LIVING IN THE PRESENCE

The Holy Spirit's agenda for you

LIVING
IN THE
PRESENCE

*The Holy Spirit's
Agenda for You*

COLIN DYE

KINGSWAY PUBLICATIONS
EASTBOURNE

First Published 1996

ISBN 0 85476 629 4

Published by Kingsway Publications Ltd, Lottbridge Drove, Eastbourne, E. Sussex BN23 6NT in association with Dovewell Publications, 45 Notting Hill Gate, London W11 3JB.
Produced and printed by Nuprint Ltd, Station Road, Harpenden, Herts, AL5 4SE, Britain.

CONTENTS

Notes on reading the Bible

In this book there are many quotations from the Bible.

The Bible is divided into 'books' with 'chapters', and the chapters have 'verses'.

Sometimes a reference is made to a particular Bible passage – e.g. John 14:16-17.

To find this passage, check the index at the front of your Bible to see where the book of John can be found.

Next you want chapter 14 in John.

Finally you turn up verses 16 to 17 in chapter 14.

You may also want to read the verses immediately in front and even afterwards, to get a clearer understanding, and to ensure that the verses have not been quoted obviously out of context.

You can read this book without a Bible, but having one to hand should make all the difference.

In some sections of the book, there are a large number of scripture references. These have been included as an aid for those readers who want to make a fuller study of the subject.

DEDICATION

For my daughter Elizabeth,
who is learning the ways of the Spirit.

INTRODUCTION

As you settle down to start reading this book, I want you to take a few minutes to think about the needs of the people who touch your life every day.

Television, radio and newspapers regularly describe some of the world's most desperate needs. They introduce us to nations which are being weakened by poverty and debt, to regions that are being devastated by war and natural disasters, to families who have been smashed by crime and accident.

We might not know personally the needy people we see on our television screens. But our hearts ache at their pain and our inability to help them.

Needs in the world

Nearer to home, we know about lives troubled by divorce, unemployment, drugs, debt, cancer, Aids, loneliness and the stress of modern-day life.

You probably know at least one person who is struggling with each of these problems. You long to reach out and help them. You can imagine what would happen if Jesus should meet them, and you wish that you shared his loving power. Yet you feel so weak and inadequate. You don't know what to do and you don't know what to say.

We all have neighbours in trouble and relatives in distress. We see the homeless and the mentally ill. We walk through housing estates where the pain and fear are so real that we can almost touch them. Then we read in the Bible about 'trampling on the works of the enemy', and feel powerless to do anything which will make a difference to the damaged lives we know so well.

Needs in the church

It's much the same in the church. Beneath hands raised in worship are lives hurting with pain. If you gaze round any congregation on a Sunday morning you can see people who are troubled by family or financial problems, by sickness or depression, by loneliness or fear. You know their pain, but feel that there is little you can do to ease it.

Then there are Christians around us who long to take a spiritual step forward, yet something always seems to hold them back. Perhaps you are even one of them yourself.

You know people who want to pray out loud, speak about Jesus, develop a ministry, see somebody healed, or conquer their worries. Maybe you pray for them – but little seems to change. Then you compare your personal experience with the stories in the New Testament – and you begin to despair.

Needs in ourselves

Somehow the needs of other people draw attention to our own inadequacy, to our lack of power and spiritual vitality.

Nearly all Christians feel God's call to reach out and

help others. We really want to ease the pain of hurting people. We long to do something about the plight of the homeless and desperately ill. We want to live and act like Jesus and the Christian people we read about in Acts. But we don't.

Deep down, we know that it can be different – that it should be different. We know that Jesus lives and acts and heals today through his body on earth. We understand that the Holy Spirit has been poured onto the church to enable all Christians to share Jesus' power and authority. We know that the Spirit's presence in our lives should make a dynamic difference to people around us.

This is what you want for yourself – to live in his dynamic holy presence – and that is why you're now reading this book.

Be ready to respond

I have written this book because I am certain that God can use *you* to make a difference to the needy folk around you.

This is not a cheap promise. I am sure because thousands of ordinary people in the church I lead in London have found God's promises in the Bible to be reliable. They are seeing God draw large numbers of needy folk to himself for lasting help and healing.

Together, we have seen over a hundred new congregations started in London. This has been possible only because our members have started to reach out effectively to the hurting men and women around them. With God's help, they are making a real difference. And, I assure you, so can you.

Our members are becoming effective witnesses only because they are living in a genuine relationship with the Spirit. If you want to minister like them, you will have to partner with the Holy Spirit. There is no other way forward.

I am delighted that you are reading this book – for it means you are open to the Spirit's influence. Now, whatever your stage of Christian development, be ready to receive fresh power and new vitality in the Holy Spirit.

Some people are so stuck in spiritual ineffectiveness that they assume their condition is normal. They think that nothing can ever change. You know that's not true. You can feel God warming your heart and breathing quiet expectancy into your life. You believe that God has led you to this book for a purpose. Please prepare to respond to the work of the Spirit in your life with willing obedience.

Be ready to be equipped

The greatest thing this book can do is help us to *know* the Holy Spirit. Not to know facts *about* him, but to know *him*.

When we are living in the presence of the all-knowing, all-powerful, all-Holy Spirit, he can activate any of his abilities in us and through us. He can do this when, where, and how he wants. Without him we will always be ineffective. With him, nothing is impossible.

As you read this book, be ready for important changes in your life. Prepare to receive a vibrant new spiritual life that you can pass on to others. Be ready to be equipped with a new release of spiritual gifts which will help you to be far more effective in ministry.

God wants to touch your life through this book. He wants to bring every aspect of Christ's abundant life to you. He wants to make you whole. He longs to set you free. Then – having received from him – his freedom and wholeness will flow from you to the needy folk around you.

Be prepared for mistakes

A secret of effective ministry is being close enough to the Spirit to hear what he is saying *and* to recognise his voice.

If a very close friend telephones, we do not need to be told who it is, for we know their voice. Likewise, we need to develop such an intimate friendship with the Spirit that we can tell the difference between his voice, the devil's voice and our own thoughts.

However, we have all made embarrassing mistakes on the 'phone. We have thought that it was one person speaking when it was someone quite different. It is the same in the spiritual realm. Nobody hears the Spirit perfectly. This means that we *all* make mistakes. Let's be ready to learn from this.

Make sure that you don't fall into either of the devil's favourite traps. Don't be so frightened of making a fool of yourself that you do nothing; and never assume that you must always have heard God accurately. I promise that you will learn most from your embarrassing failures! I do! So prepare for mistakes and make sure that you benefit from them.

Begin to submit

As I write this book, my greatest prayer for you is that you will submit yourself completely to the work and presence of the Holy Spirit in your life.

This will not be something which happens by accident. God will not make you submit to him. You must decide. It has to be a conscious act of your will – one that you go on making every day of your life.

In fact, the degree to which you submit to the leadership and the initiative of the Spirit is the degree to which the Spirit can reveal Christ through your life.

If the Holy Spirit asks us to do something – no matter how trivial or demanding – he will always supply everything we need to carry out his task. We need to hear his voice, obey his command, and then depend entirely on his provision.

Submitting to the Spirit does not mean only obeying his *every* prompting, it also means *never* acting on our own initiative. Presumption is just as wrong and unhelpful as disobedience! If God does not tell us to do something, no amount of effort on our part will ever achieve it.

We are called to live in his presence and become true partners with the Spirit. Our part is to provide the arms, legs, mouth, touch, voice, and so on. His part is to direct and enable. We cannot control or manipulate God. He works through us. He uses us. But he does not do this mechanically, over-riding our free will.

We have to co-operate with the Spirit as a genuine partner in the task of taking God's healing love to the hurting world where we live.

Time for a change

The broken lives we see on television screens, the damaged people we pass on the streets, our bruised neighbours and friends – these folk don't realise it, but they all need to be changed by the loving power of the Holy Spirit.

The world has had enough of religion without power. It is repulsed by religion without purity. Yet Jesus Christ – the perfect example of full power and total purity – is still alive. And he is working in the world through his church.

Jesus is looking for men and women who will turn away from human reasoning and worldly methods. He is seeking people who will live always in complete dependence on the Holy Spirit. He wants you. He wants you to live for

14

him, for him alone. Jesus is calling you to share the life of his precious Holy Spirit.

You know that it is time for a change in your life. It is time for you to move into the permanent presence of the Spirit. Now is God's time for you to start living in purity and in power. Not for your sake, but so that our needy world can feel God's saving love and healing touch.

PART ONE

WHO IS THE HOLY SPIRIT?

Many ordinary people are puzzled when Christians talk about the Holy Spirit. They understand what we mean by God the Father. They have heard about Jesus the Son. But they are baffled when we mention the Holy Spirit.

They don't realise that we are talking about a real person – a 'he' not an 'it' – who is dynamically alive. Instead, they think that we are trying to describe some sort of vague presence or nice religious ghost.

Some Christians are equally uncertain about the Holy Spirit. They know that he is God, but they're not sure what he does or is like. So, in the first part of this book, I will outline the Bible's teaching about the Holy Spirit. This should help us start to know him rather better than we do.

The Spirit in the Old Testament

We all know the name 'Holy Spirit'. But some believers may be surprised to learn that this expression appears only twice in the Old Testament. These two important passages are a good starting point for our study.

Psalm 51 deals with repentance in a powerful fashion. The writer – probably David – is deeply sorry for his sin and, in verse 11, he begs God for the Holy Spirit.

If the writer's request for the 'Holy' Spirit is successful, he promises that he will tell sinners the way to God *and* that he will praise the Lord with his mouth.

> **The 'Holy' Spirit is associated with repentant lives, sharing the good news about God, powerful signs and special direction**

Isaiah 63:10 shows that the Holy Spirit is grieved whenever we turn away from God: this is the opposite of repentance.

Read this chapter now and see how it links the presence of the Holy Spirit with signs, wonders and with miraculous guidance.

Immediately we can see that the 'Holy' Spirit in the Old Testament is associated with repentant lives, with sharing the good news about God, *and* with powerful signs and special direction.

MYSTERIOUS PICTURES

Throughout the rest of the Old Testament, the Holy Spirit is called 'the Spirit' or 'the Spirit of God'. He is also described in a series of unusual images which help us begin to grasp his character and appreciate his activities.

Wind

The Old Testament was written in the Hebrew language. The Hebrew word for 'spirit' is *ruach*, and this is a word which also means 'wind'.

In many places *ruach* describes a wind which is immensely powerful, even destructive. But it is always under God's control and it always effects his will.

> The Spirit is a hurricane whom we cannot control or predict. He is an invading force who transforms wherever he blows. He is God's power in action

The Spirit is a hurricane whom we cannot control or predict. He is an invading force who transforms wherever he blows. He is God's power in action.

The following passages give us an insight into this picture of the Spirit. Genesis 8:1; Exodus 10:13, 14:21; 1 Kings 19:11; Job 21:18; Psalm 1:4, 35:5; 104:3; 107:25; 135:7; Ezekiel 37:9; Amos 4:13.

Breath

Ruach also means 'breath'. The Spirit is the wind which comes straight from God's mouth. He is 'the breath of God' – the breath without which men and women are dead.

Ruach literally means breathing out through the nose with great violence. This isn't a picture of the Spirit as a gentle

> The Spirit is the breath without which men and women are dead

breeze or a quiet wheeze. It is a picture of God taking a deep breath and blowing as hard as he can! Read Ezekiel

37:1-14 and see how the Spirit, God's breath, changes dead people into a powerful army!

Water

The Bible often uses water as a symbol of God's blessing and spiritual refreshment.

In Ezekiel 47:1-12, the prophet saw water flowing out from the heart of God's future temple. This vision of pure water represented the unrestricted flow of God's blessings to his people. See how Ezekiel was ordered to go on immersing himself deeper and deeper in the water!

Jeremiah 2:13 & 17:13 describe God as a 'fountain of living waters', and John 7:37-39 tells us that this is a picture of the Holy Spirit.

We know that water is essential to life. We all die very quickly without it. In olden times, armies usually tried to cut off the water supply whenever they attacked an enemy.

> We all die very quickly without water

Water is also vital for washing. It naturally purifies us, and was used ceremonially in the Bible to consecrate Priests and Levites (Exodus 29:4; Numbers 8:7) and to remove defilement from all people (Leviticus 11:40; 15:5-33). In Ezekiel 36: 25-28 God promises to clean us with water and make brand new people of us.

These verses help to build up a picture of the Spirit's activity. He is God's ultimate blessing. We are lifeless without him. We need his living water to make us clean.

Fire

Fire is even more effective than water at purifying and refining. In the Old Testament, fire was a symbol of God's intervention in history and of his Spirit purifying hearts.

When God appeared to people, he was often surrounded by fire (Exodus 3:2, 13:21; 19:18; Deuteronomy 4:11-12).

Fire also revealed God's presence, his holiness, his judgement and his anger against sin (2 Kings 6:17; Deuteronomy 4:24; Isaiah 66:15; Zechariah 13:9).

Isaiah 4:2-6 clearly shows that 'the spirit of burning' is a vital part of God's purifying work. Read the passage and grasp that we all need to be cleansed by the Spirit's fire if we are to become holy.

We need to be cleansed by the Spirit's fire if we are to become holy

Oil

In Old Testament days, oil was used practically to prepare food, to provide light and to aid healing. It was also used ceremoniously to anoint priests and kings. It is this *anointing* which is another picture of the Spirit.

The anointing with oil symbolised the equipping of a priest or king for service with the necessary resource of God's Spirit. We can read about this in 1 Samuel 10:1-9; 16:13; Isaiah 61:1 and Zechariah 4:1-14.

When oil was poured over priests and kings as a picture of the Spirit, it showed that the Spirit would feed, enlighten and heal through the anointed person. Isaiah 61:1-3 shows this very clearly.

Anointing with oil symbolised the priest's equipping for service with the necessary resource of God's Spirit

Dove

Today, we tend to think that doves signify gentleness. But they had a different meaning in Bible days. Doves were used then as a source of food and to carry messages.

The dove in Genesis 8:1-12 announced the new creation

and a new existence in the promises of God. The dove is revealed as the King's bride in Song of Songs 2:14, 5:2 & 6:9. Leviticus 5:7-10 shows the dove as an acceptable sacrifice for poor people.

> The dove showed that Jesus was the messenger who would feed God's people

The Hebrew word for dove is *Yonah*. Jonah was the messenger of God who was sent on a mission to speak to sinners, and who spent three days in a fish's belly before his resurrection.

This suggests that, when the Spirit came down like a dove at Jesus' baptism, there was no picture of gentleness. Instead, the dove showed that Jesus was a messenger who would feed God's people. The dove revealed the dawn of a new creation and the sacrifice for poor people's sins.

A PERSON

Although all these Old Testament word-pictures about the Spirit are impersonal, they are appropriate images for an immensely powerful being. Taken together, the pictures point us towards a person whom we will see more clearly in the New Testament.

> The Holy Spirit is at work whenever we see God demonstrating his power in the Old Testament

These unusual images also help us to visualise some of God's dynamic activities. They enable us to begin to appreciate that the Spirit brings both power and purity.

Using a modern word-picture, we can think of the Holy Spirit as the Chief Executive of the Godhead. A company's chief executive is responsible for implementing the policies, programmes, decisions and vision of the directors.

So the Holy Spirit acts on the Father's behalf to implement his will.

This means that the Holy Spirit is at work when we see God demonstrating his power in the Old Testament, and whenever people return to spiritual and personal purity.

THE SPIRIT'S WORK

The phrase 'the Spirit of God' appears nearly one hundred times in the Old Testament. Every time it describes God at work, God bringing change, God making a difference to his world and his people. The Spirit really is God's power in action.

The Old Testament shows that the Spirit is involved in four broad areas of activity. He moulds and animates creation. He reveals God's truth to his servants the prophets. He awakens people to God. And he equips some men and women for special service.

Creating

The first fact that the Bible teaches us about the Spirit is his role in creation.

Genesis 1:1-2 states, 'In the beginning God created the heavens and the earth. The earth was without form, and void; and darkness was on the face of the deep. And the Spirit of God was hovering over the face of the waters.'

This means that the Holy Spirit hovered over the waters, like a mother hen broods over her eggs bringing them to life.

Later in the creation story, we read that 'the Lord God formed man of the dust of the ground, and breathed into his nostrils the breath of life; and man became a living being (Genesis 2:7).

What the Father created, the Spirit animated. The

Spirit, the very breath of God, released God's life-giving power and dust became living humanity.

Job 26:13; 33:4; Psalm 33:6; 104:29-30; Isaiah 34:16 & 40:7 illustrate the Holy Spirit's involvement in creating and sustaining life.

Revealing

The Scriptures teach a very strong association between the Spirit and the revelation of God's truth and will to his messengers the prophets. This is the basis of prophecy.

Moses' wish in Numbers 11:29 is the first hint of a link between the Spirit and prophecy. Saul's experiences in 1 Samuel 10 and 19:18-24 show that the Spirit's descent led to spontaneous prophecy. Micah 3:8 suggests that the Spirit not only supplied the inspiration but also gave the courage to deliver the revelation. And Joel 2:28 makes it clear that the coming of the Spirit should result in prophetic speech.

In Ezekiel 37:1-2, it was the Spirit who brought the prophet to the valley of dry bones and revealed God's truths to Ezekiel through a vision.

The Spirit brought the prophet to the valley and revealed God's truths to him through a dynamic vision

Many other verses show the Spirit revealing God's truth by distilled insight or direct communication. For example: Numbers 24:2; 2 Samuel 23:2; 1 Chronicles 12:18; 2 Chronicles 15:1; Nehemiah 9:30; Job 32:8; Isaiah 61:1-4; Ezekiel 2:2; 11:24; Zechariah 7:12.

In a few passages, the Spirit teaches God's truth to a wider group of people than just the prophets. For example: Nehemiah 9:20; Psalms 143:10; Isaiah 48:16; 63:10-14.

Awakening

Throughout the Old Testament, we can read about the Spirit waking men and women to the reality of God. He convicts people about their sin. He leads them to repentance and faith. He urges them towards righteousness. And he encourages them to respond to God with praise and prayer.

In Psalm 51, David cries out to God about his sin. It seems that he has been convicted and brought to repentance by the Spirit.

In Psalm 51, David cries out about his sin. He has been convicted and brought to repentance by the Holy Spirit

Verses 10-12 show how the Spirit has alerted David to spiritual reality and drawn a response from him. 'Create in me a clean heart, O God, and renew a steadfast spirit within me. Do not cast me away from your presence and do not take your Holy Spirit from me. Restore to me the joy of your salvation, and uphold me with your generous Spirit.'

Isaiah 44:3-5 illustrates how the Spirit causes people to turn to God. 'I will pour my Spirit on your descendants... One will say, "I am the Lord's". Another will call himself by the name of Jacob. Another will write with his hand, "The Lord's" and name himself by the name of Israel.'

The book of Ezekiel teaches us much about the work of the Spirit. Ezekiel 39:29 shows that the Spirit reveals God's own face to us, and 11:19-20 & 36:25-27 make plain the difference that the Spirit makes in our lives.

Joel 2:28-32 dramatically lists some changes in human lives when the Spirit comes with life and power. Children prophesy. The elderly dream. Uneducated servants see visions. Many, many people are saved and delivered.

Equipping

The Scriptures show us that one of the Spirit's main Old Testament activities was equipping people for leadership.

In Genesis 41:33-42, Pharaoh chose Joseph as his leader for Egypt because he recognised that God's Spirit had given Joseph special discernment and wisdom.

Numbers 11:16-29 makes it clear that the same Spirit which equipped Moses for national leadership was needed by the seventy elders for their leadership responsibilities.

The Spirit enabled *judges* like Joshua, Othniel, Gideon, Jephthah and Samson to lead Israel and to deliver them from enemies (Judges 3:10; 6:34; 11:29; 13:25; 14:19; 15:14).

Saul and David, the first two *kings*, were personally chosen by God as rulers – later ones merely followed the family line. These two were helped by the Spirit to rule Israel effectively (1 Samuel 10:10; 11:6; 16:13; 19:20-23).

People could only function as *prophets* if they were called, inspired and empowered by the Spirit. God called them into his presence to reveal his intentions, and to commission and equip them with the vital resource of his Holy Spirit.

> **People could only function as *prophets* if they were called, inspired and empowered by the Spirit**

Although Isaiah 42:1-4 does point forward to the supreme prophet, Jesus, it also describes a prophet of Isaiah's day. 'My Servant whom I uphold... I have put my Spirit upon him; he will bring forth justice to the Gentiles.'

Prophets were known as God's servants throughout the Old Testament. And this servant – who is mentioned several times in Isaiah – had clearly been equipped with the Spirit for the task God had given him. People were also equipped by the Spirit with skill and strength for creative work.

Exodus 31:1-3 & 35:30-35 show how Bezaleel was 'filled with the Spirit of God, in wisdom, in understanding, in knowledge, and in all manner of workmanship'.

The Spirit gave Bezaleel all sorts of skills and abilities in craftwork to help him build a beautiful Tabernacle. Haggai 2:4-9 & Zechariah 4:6-10

> The Spirit gave Bezaleel all sorts of skills and abilities in craftwork to help him build a beautiful Tabernacle

show that Zerubbabel was also equipped by the Spirit to build a lovely building for God.

It is likely that Bezaleel and Zerubbabel were already talented workers before the Spirit came upon them. But the Spirit can give people extra-special ability in order to serve God even better.

A FORESHADOWING

Exodus 31:3 uses a phrase for receiving the Spirit that we find many more times in the New Testament. Many biblical truths are only partially revealed in the Old Testament: this is called a 'foreshadowing'. We get a valuable insight into a particular truth in the Old Testament, and then see the full picture in the New Testament.

We would not know the Spirit very well if we based our understanding of him only on the Old Testament scriptures. We might think that he is merely an extension or dimension of God.

But the New Testament makes it absolutely clear that the Spirit is not just a power. He is a person. He is a member of the Godhead in his own right. The Holy Spirit is the third person of the Trinity. He is God the Holy Spirit.

The Spirit in the Gospels

The New Testament was written in the Greek language. The Greek word for Spirit is *pneuma*, and it also carries the meaning of a powerful wind as well as a personal spirit.

In the New Testament, Jesus and the apostles recognise that the Old Testament picture language referred to the third person of the Godhead. They understood that references to God's breath meant the Spirit's personal activity.

In Mark 12:36, Jesus says that David spoke by the Holy Spirit. In Luke 4:18-21, Jesus claims that his preaching fulfills Isaiah's witness to his own anointing. And in John 3:5-10, Jesus rebukes Nicodemus for not realising that his teaching on the new birth of 'water and the Spirit' looks back to Ezekiel 36:25-27.

John's announcement

Anybody who knows nothing about Jesus, who turns to the Gospels for information, is faced with John's announcement that Jesus 'will baptize you with the Holy Spirit and fire'. This is recorded in Matthew 3:1-12; Mark 1:1-8 and Luke 3:1-18. John 1:19-34 uses slightly different wording; but all four gospels show that, as far as John the Baptist was concerned, the single most important task Jesus would perform would be to baptize in the Holy Spirit.

John drew a parallel between his baptizing in water and the Stronger One's baptizing in Spirit and fire. Just as the crowds were immersed in water by John, so Jesus' followers would be immersed in the Holy Spirit and in fire.

This must have been a wonderful promise for John's listeners – who knew the Old Testament so well. What glorious pictures must have rushed through their minds. A baptism in God's hurricane, in his oil, in his living water.

An immersion in the holy breath which inspired and equipped the prophets and kings.

Surely this baptism would bring miracles, praise, proclamation, prophecy, service and kingly authority to all who were immersed in the Spirit by Jesus. John's listeners must have tingled with excitement as their minds raced through the acts of the Spirit in the Old Testament.

But the people who heard John's announcement would also have been challenged – even frightened – by his mention of a baptism in fire. They would have known passages like Isaiah 1:25, Daniel 7:10, Zechariah 13:9 and Malachi 3:2-3 which describe the Spirit coming to purify hearts.

They may have thought of Isaiah 4:3-6, for it is so close to John's announcement. 'It shall come to pass that he who is left in Zion and he who remains

> John expected this baptism in the Spirit by Jesus to provide both hurricane power *and* holy purity

in Jerusalem will be called holy... When the Lord has washed away the filth of the daughters of Zion, and purged the blood of Jerusalem from her midst, by the spirit of judgment and by the spirit of burning.'

John's baptism can wash, but Jesus' will purify. John's wipes the slate clean, but Jesus' transforms the very slate.

Whichever Gospel we read, John's announcement introduces us both to Jesus and to the Holy Spirit. However, we can only understand his announcement in the light of the Old Testament. And in that light, it is plain that John expected this baptism in the Spirit by Jesus to provide both hurricane power *and* holy purity.

Luke's phrase

We've seen that Exodus 31:3 describes Bezaleel as being 'filled with the Spirit'. Luke uses the same phrase again and again in both his Gospel and in Acts – which it seems that he also wrote.

Luke uses the phrase to describe what happened to ordinary people like Elizabeth and Zachariah (Luke 1:41, 67) as well as to people like John and Jesus (Luke 1:15; 4:1). He uses the same expression a further seven times in the book of Acts (2:4; 4:8; 6:5; 7:55; 9:17; 11:23 & 13:52).

> We are plunged by Jesus into the Holy Spirit to be filled with the Spirit like a sponge – so that the Spirit is in us and we are in the Spirit

The Greek word Luke uses for 'to fill' is *pletho*. This is the Greek word which is used in Matthew 27:48 and John 19:29 to describe the way a sponge was filled with sour wine for Jesus.

There, at the cross, a dry sponge was immersed in a jar full of wine. The wine was not poured into the sponge; instead the sponge was filled by being placed into the wine. This is how we are filled with the Holy Spirit.

We are not cups which are occasionally 'topped up' with the Holy Spirit. We do not contain the Spirit. Instead, we are plunged by Jesus into the Holy Spirit to be filled like a sponge being filled with liquid. We are saturated by the Spirit, we are filled with the Spirit, because we are placed *into* the Spirit to start living in the presence of the Spirit.

Luke uses the same phrase to describe *both* the experience of becoming filled *and* the result of being filled (Luke 1:41 & 4:1; Acts 2:4 & 4:8). This means that we remain filled with the Spirit for as long as we remain living in the Holy Spirit.

Jesus' ministry

The Gospels show that Jesus' life was lived in the Holy Spirit from his earliest earthly moments. Matthew 1:18-21 and Luke 1:31-35 both show how Jesus was conceived by the Holy Spirit.

Although Jesus was fully divine, he did not cling to his equality with God but emptied himself instead. He laid aside his majesty and picked up the mantle of humility. He put down his omnipotence and his omnipresence and put on all the human weaknesses except sin.

He did not cease to be God – because he could not give up his divine nature and attributes – rather he sacrificed the public treatment and honour due to him because he was God and assumed the condition of a human slave.

This meant that he grew up and worked as a carpenter with few people noticing any power or special qualities. Because he had taken on the form of humanity, Jesus needed to be filled with the Spirit before he could commence his ministry.

Jesus' baptism by John was the moment of his commissioning and equipping for ministry. As he rose from the river, Matthew 3:13-17 reports that the Spirit came down like a dove and that God announced, 'This is my beloved Son, in whom I am well pleased'.

> Although Jesus was fully divine, he did not cling to his equality with God but emptied himself instead

This was Jesus' anointing and equipping for service. Mark 1:12-13 shows that the first act of the Spirit was to drive Jesus into the desert for a dramatic battle with the evil one. Luke 4:1 states that Jesus was 'filled with the Spirit' when he entered the wilderness, but Luke 4:14 reports that he was 'in the power of the Spirit' when he left the wilderness and returned to Galilee.

There is a critical difference between being filled with the Spirit and being filled with the power of the Spirit. The former is the basic condition. The latter is the result of the condition being lived out in obedience within temptation. Jesus' spiritual purity in the face of demonic temptation resulted in his spiritual power.

> There is a critical difference between being filled with the Spirit and being filled with the power of the Spirit

Luke 4:16-27 describes how Jesus went from the wilderness to the Nazareth synagogue, quoted from Isaiah 61, and applied it to himself. At the river, he had been anointed to serve. Acts 10:38 reflects on this anointing and states that – once and for all – God became 'with him' in a clear demonstration of power.

Because of his anointing with the Holy Spirit, Jesus was enabled to do that which – as a man – he had previously been unable to do. He 'went about doing good and healing all who were oppressed by the devil'.

The whole of Jesus' ministry was shot through with the Spirit. The Holy Spirit was the source of his life, his power and his emotions. He was filled with joy by the Spirit, Luke 10:21; he drove out demons by the Spirit, Matthew 12:28; taught by the Spirit, Acts 1:2; and sacrificed himself by the Spirit, Hebrews 9:14.

His life, growth, character, emotions and ministry were all the result of his being born of the Spirit, his being filled with the Holy Spirit, and his continued living in the Spirit.

Another the same

Jesus taught little about the Spirit until the Last Supper. The apostles were sad that Jesus was leaving them, so Jesus explained it was better for them that he left: 'It is to your advantage that I go away; for if I do not go away, the Helper [Greek *parakletos*, 'Paraclete'] will not come to you; but if I depart, I will send him to you' (John 16:7).

Jesus referred to the Spirit as the 'Paraclete' five times during the Last

The Spirit is just like Jesus!

Supper (John 13-17). In John 14:16, he uses a special Greek word for 'another' which underlines that the Spirit is another similar, not another different, to Jesus. This means that the Spirit is just like Jesus!

It is very hard to translate 'Paraclete' into English. Most versions of the Bible use a different word: for example, Counsellor, Advocate, Helper, Comforter or Encourager.

The word comes from *parakaleo* – which means 'to call alongside'. So the Holy Spirit is called alongside us, and he calls from alongside us. He comes alongside to help us, to speak for us, to comfort, encourage and advise us. He helps in exactly the same way as Jesus!

The Holy Spirit is called alongside us, and he calls from alongside us

John 14:25-27 reveals him as teacher, and John 15:26 states that he will bear witness to Jesus: the Spirit is 'The Witness', our witness is a secondary witness which underlines his. John 16:7-11 points to his activity in the world, and John 16:13 promises that the Spirit will lead disciples into complete truth.

However, the essence of the Spirit's work is kept for the end of the Last Supper. In John 16:14-15, Jesus explains that the Spirit 'will glorify me'. Everything the Spirit says and does is to glorify, to illuminate, to floodlight, to focus the world's attention on Jesus.

The humble Holy Spirit never draws attention to himself. He always remains in the background, ensuring that all glory and attention goes to Jesus. When people are really filled with the Holy Spirit, they will surely behave like him.

The beginning of the Church

The introduction to the 'Paraclete' in the upper room was Jesus' last message before his death at Calvary. Three days later, he burst from the tomb and walked through locked doors to thrill the apostles.

His first words were so like Genesis 2:7 and Ezekiel 37:5-9: 'Peace to you! As the Father has sent me, I also send you. And when he had said this he breathed on them, and said to them, "Receive the Holy Spirit"' (John 20:20-22).

It appears that this was a prophetic action by Jesus which was fulfilled at Pentecost. Jesus had been sent into the world by the Father when the Spirit came upon Mary, so he sent the church into the world here in a similar way. Just as Jesus had to wait until his baptism for God's power, so the church would have to wait until Pentecost for the power.

> Just as Jesus had to wait until his baptism for the power, so the church would have to wait until Pentecost

Jesus' last words before Calvary, his first words after the resurrection, and his last words before his ascension, were all about the Holy Spirit. In Acts 1:1-8, he reminded the disciples about John's announcement; and – just before ascending – he promised them that, 'You shall receive power when the Holy Spirit has come upon you; and you shall be witnesses to me...'

Those were Jesus' last words. The church, which — as

Ephesians 2:11-18 shows – had begun at Calvary some forty days before, was soon to be filled with the Spirit and empowered for active service.

The Spirit in the Early Church

In the New Testament, the early church leaders introduce the Holy Spirit as the third member of the Trinity. They make it plain that he is both fully personal and fully divine.

FULLY PERSONAL, FULLY GOD

If 'the Holy Spirit' was merely a way of describing God's power, the New Testament would not continually name the Spirit as a 'him' rather than an 'it'. It would not show him acting in such a thoroughly personal manner.

For example, the New Testament reveals that the Holy Spirit hears, speaks, helps, witnesses, convinces, convicts, commands, tells, declares, leads, guides, grieves, teaches, forbids, opposes, desires, gives speech, and intercedes for believers. Surely he could do none of these things if he were not a full person in his own right.

We can read about these personal activities in John 14:26; 15:26; 16:7-15; Acts 2:4; 5:3-4; 8:29; 13:2; 16:6-7; Romans 8:14-27; Galatians 4:6; 5:17-18; Ephesians 4:30.

If 'the Holy Spirit' was just another way of describing God's presence, the New Testament would not make it so clear that he is God, yet distinct from the Father and Son.

Passages like Matthew 28:19; Acts 5:3-4; 1 Corinthians 12:4-6; 2 Corinthians 13:14; Ephesians 1:3-14; 2:18; 3:14-19; 4:4-6; 2 Thessalonians 2:13-14; 1 Peter 1:2 & Revelation 1:4-5 link the Father, the Son and the Spirit together in a way which leaves no room for doubt: the Spirit really is

Almighty God. And he made his grand appearance on the Day of Pentecost.

PENTECOST

For Jews in Jesus' day, the feast of Pentecost celebrated the end of the first phase of the harvest. The very first fruits had been picked. The latter rain had fallen. They looked forward to three dry, hot, hard-working months of summer when they would reap the golden harvest.

> The house was the baptistry. The disciples were the candidates. Jesus was the baptizer. The Spirit was the element

When we understand this background, we can grasp why God chose Pentecost to empower the Church. It was time for harvest, and they needed the Spirit's help to gather it in.

Acts 2:1-41 tells the story of that great day. Jesus had told the disciples to stay in Jerusalem until they received the promised power. They obeyed, and Jesus kept his promise.

The language of Pentecost in Acts 2 is similar both to Jesus' baptism and to some of Ezekiel's visions. 'Suddenly there came a sound from heaven, as of a rushing mighty wind, and it filled the whole house where they were sitting. Then there appeared to them forked tongues, as of fire, and one sat on each of them.'

These manifestations of the Spirit were a vision of fire and wind rather than physical events. Unusual events – like the forked tongues – are often associated with the Spirit's coming, but they neither measure nor cause the transformation which takes place when the Spirit comes.

Today, people often focus on the physical phenomena

rather than on the Spirit. Strange things frequently occur, but the spiritual change he brings is what matters the most.

At Pentecost, the house was the baptistry. The disciples were the candidates. Jesus was the baptizer. The Holy Spirit – the wind and the fire of God – was the element. 'And they were all filled with the Holy Spirit'.

Life in the Spirit had begun. The day that Joel had prophesied, that Moses had longed for, had finally arrived.

The fire

The tongues of fire were a reminder of the first Temple's consecration in 2 Chronicles 7:1-3 – when fire fell from heaven and the glory of God filled the house of God. The fire showed that God had come to live in an earthly home.

This happened again at Pentecost. God's new temple, made of flesh and blood, not bricks and mortar, had been formed by the breath and blood of Jesus at Passover.

On the day of Pentecost, the Spirit's fire fell and the new human temple was purified, dedicated, surrounded by glory and filled with God's power and presence.

> The Spirit came to reveal the presence and character of God, and to commission the church with a task

Here was the pillar of fire to guide the church through the dark days ahead. Jesus had promised that the Paraclete would lead them. He had come to do this.

Here was the fire which had blazed in a bush but not consumed it – that burning revelation to Moses of the presence and character of God, that commission which would take Moses the rest of his life to fulfil.

The Spirit's fire came at Pentecost to reveal the presence

and character of God, and to commission the church with a task which would take to the end of time to perform.

And here was the fire which had purified Isaiah's lips and provided him with words to speak to the people. So the church received the gift of Spirit-inspired speech to witness to Jesus – just as Jesus had promised. The Paraclete had been called alongside to help the disciples to witness.

> **Pentecost proved that Jesus had ascended and taken his place at the Father's right hand**

The wind

The sound of the mighty rushing wind revealed that God's Spirit-wind was blowing again.

He had been active in creation. He had dried the waters of the flood to usher in a new age. He had divided the Red Sea to allow the Jews to enter the new land of promise. He had created a mighty army out of a valley of dry bones.

The hurricane of God's Spirit now blew into the church. He came alongside to breath energy and power, to bring new order and turn raw recruits into an army. All this, and more, took place when the Holy Spirit came at Pentecost.

THE NEW AGE

The first result was that the disciples 'were all filled with the Holy Spirit and began to speak in other tongues, as the Spirit gave them utterance'. They experienced a measure of what Jesus had experienced following his baptism and the Spirit's descent upon him.

Some of the Jews who were watching thought that the disciples had to be drunk. People are often suspicious of the phenomena which can be associated with the coming of the Spirit. But the disciples' experience was not due to alcohol, or to extreme emotions – it was an initiation into a new dimension of living. Life in the Spirit had begun.

Life in the Spirit

Peter stood before the crowd of Jews and explained that what had happened was what had been prophesied by Joel. God had finally poured out his Spirit upon them.

However Pentecost was the day of *first* fruits. This was the first installment, not the total package. The harvest of God's Spirit had begun, but it was far from over.

Peter did not claim that Joel's prophecy had been completely fulfilled at Pentecost. He merely explained that it was what Joel had spoken about.

The Joel 2:28-32 prophecy was fulfilled only in the experience of the people actually present at Pentecost. However the possibility of the prophecy being fulfilled in the experience of all humanity came into being. The Spirit's coming at Pentecost was just the first fruit. There was much, much more to come.

Jesus is proclaimed

Pentecost was about Jesus. Today, when the church celebrates Pentecost, believers often speak and sing about the Spirit. But all of the Spirit's genuine activities rivet attention on Jesus – he does not draw attention to himself.

Once Peter had finished quoting from Joel, he launched into the first Pentecost sermon. 'Men of Israel, hear these words: Jesus of Nazarcth...' With the Spirit's help, Peter preached about Jesus. Three thousand people responded – this was the difference that the Spirit had made.

At Pentecost, the risen Christ did what John had promised. He baptized in the Holy Spirit and fire. The focus is on the baptizer, not the element. The outpouring of

> **All the Spirit's activities rivet attention on Jesus – he does not draw any attention to himself**

the Spirit showed that Jesus had ascended and taken his place in heaven at the Father's right hand. It proved that Jesus was alive!

Pentecost was the incarnation of the Spirit into the church. Through the Spirit's coming, the church could do all that Christ would have done had he remained on earth – only more so.

From that day of first fruits, the Spirit's work of glorifying Jesus has gone on through the church. It continues through long years of patient reaping, and will not end until the harvest is completed and the Lord of the harvest returns in power and great glory.

The Age of the Spirit

Ever since that Day of Pentecost, the church has been living in what is called 'the Age of the Spirit'. There is much talk today about a 'New Age', but this has nothing to do with the Age of the Spirit in which we exist as Christians.

The Jews who lived at the time of Jesus believed that a Messiah would come who would bring in God's Kingdom and deal with all evil powers. They did not recognize Jesus as God, partly because he did not establish God's Kingdom in its final form. Even now, that is still to happen at some point in the future.

This can seem confusing. Everyday experience tells us that our age is an evil age which is dominated by Satan. Yet Jesus stated in Matthew 12:28 that God's Kingdom was already here, and then he also prayed in Matthew 6:10 for the Kingdom to come.

This means that there must be an overlap – and it is this overlap which we call the 'Church Age' or the 'Age of the Spirit'. The Kingdom of God is present during our current evil age, but it will not be fully established on earth – with an end to all evil – until Jesus returns to rule in person.

Although Jesus is already the King of kings, we know that he is absent from earth. One day he will return, but at

> **The Kingdom of God is present, but it will not be fully established until Jesus returns in person**

the moment he rules here by the Holy Spirit – which is why we call it 'the Age of the Spirit'.

During this current age, it is down to us to get on with the job of establishing God's Kingdom on earth and resisting the powers of darkness. We can only do this with the help of the Holy Spirit.

Open to all

The 'Church Age' – or 'Age of the Spirit' – is different from the period before Pentecost that we read about in the Old Testament. One main difference is the total availability of the Spirit for all people who serve the living God.

Until Pentecost, the Spirit was given only to a special few believers – mainly to prophets, judges and some kings. Numbers 11:16-30 describes how Moses needed help, but his burden could only be shared with those on whom the Spirit came. This was restricted to seventy male elders.

In verse 29, an exasperated Moses exclaimed, 'Oh that all the Lord's people were prophets and that the Lord would put his Spirit upon them'. Joel 2:28-29 looked forward to a day when God would do exactly that. And God kept his promise at Pentecost when he poured out his Spirit without restriction upon the church.

> There is no limitation on the giving of the Spirit, and no restriction on the receiving. In this 'Age of the Spirit', every believer can receive the Holy Spirit

On the day of Pentecost, there was no limitation on the giving of the Spirit by God, and no restriction on the receiving by believers.

Since then, right through the 'Age of the Spirit', every single Christian disciple has been able to receive the Holy Spirit. Every aspect of the Spirit's character and power has always been available to every believer.

Continuous witness

The 'Age of the Spirit' is characterized by the Spirit's witness to Jesus. Before the Spirit came, God's people – the Jews – were not concerned with persuading other nations to turn to the living God.

However, since Pentecost, the Spirit has continuously borne witness to Jesus, given glory to Jesus, and focused the world's attention on the only Son of God.

It has been said that 'the church exists for mission as a fire exists for burning'. Preaching, evangelism, witnessing, loving good works, missionary activity, church planting – all these have been central to the Age of the Spirit as the witnessing Holy Spirit has shone his spotlight on Jesus.

Right through 'the Church Age', the Spirit has prompted Christian believers to add their witness to his. He has inspired millions of disciples to live and speak in a way which has power-fully proclaimed the good news about Jesus to their nation and culture.

> The church exists for mission as a fire exists for burning

Holy lifestyle

Please remember that water is a very important biblical picture of the Spirit, and then go on to grasp the significance of the fact that water *always* seeks out the lowest place. So the Holy Spirit is always self-effacing.

Throughout his Age, instead of drawing attention to himself, he has always pointed people to the Son and to the Father. This holy humility is an important characteristic of those people who are truly controlled by the Holy Spirit.

In Galatians 5:16-26, Paul contrasts 'the works of the flesh' with 'the fruit of the Spirit'. He shows that the lifestyle of those who are led by the Spirit in his Age is 'love, joy, peace, long-suffering, kindness, goodness, faithfulness, gentleness and self-control'.

> Humility is an important characteristic of people who are truly controlled by the Holy Spirit

Paul makes plain that 'hatred, contentions, jealousies, outbursts of wrath, selfish ambitions, dissensions and envy' are fundamentally opposed to the Spirit.

Churches today need to understand that the Age of the Spirit is an age when they are meant to be characterized by the Spirit's humility, meekness, patience, lowliness and peace.

Basic truth

Jesus taught that 'the Helper, the Holy Spirit, whom the Father will send in my name, will teach you all things, and bring to your remembrance all things that I said to you' (John 14:26).

Jesus also said that the Spirit of truth 'will guide you into all truth; for he will not speak on his own authority, but whatever he hears he will speak' (John 16:13).

This means that the Age of the Spirit is an age when truth really matters. This is why sermons have always been central, and why books and tapes are increasingly important. Ever since the day of Pentecost, the Spirit has been acting as the church's teacher – gently guiding us towards the truth.

Looking back through history, we can see how the Spirit has highlighted aspects of truth in different ages.

The Spirit of truth has focused on big broad themes like monastic simplicity and pioneer evangelism, justification by grace, personal faith, every-member ministry, overseas missions, the unity of the body, spiritual gifts, and so on.

> He teaches quietly and patiently – we often miss his activity, but he never gives up

This teacher is gentle and meek, not harsh and cruel. He teaches us quietly and patiently – we may miss his activity, but he never gives up on us. He constantly draws us away from those small unimportant details which seem to fascinate us, back to the Spirit's large basic themes which matter the most in God's kingdom.

Spiritual gifts

When Moses longed for all God's people to prophecy, he was yearning for the Spirit to enable God's people to function at a higher – a *super*natural – level.

This is precisely what the Spirit has been doing since Pentecost in the 'Church Age'. Right through the centuries, he has given 'gifts' to God's people which have helped them to carry out the task of establishing God's kingdom on earth.

The New Testament describes these gifts in different ways. However, Romans 12:3-13, 1 Corinthians 12:1-11 and Ephesians 4:1-13 show that 'spiritual gifts' are given to help *all* of God's people to witness, to worship and to work for God's kingdom. These gifts are not reserved for a few.

> Spiritual gifts are given to help *all* of God's people to witness, to worship and to work for God's kingdom

Some believers have misused these gifts. Others have preferred to argue about them than to use them to bless and build others. But the gifts are not given for entertainment or argument. They are tools to get the job done!

Some leaders have argued that the Spirit stopped giving his gifts at the end of the New Testament era. Historical records, however, describe some use of all the supernatural spiritual gifts in every century since Pentecost.

And the church's experience in the last twenty years – right round the globe – demonstrates beyond doubt that spiritual gifts are a key feature of the present age.

Constant change

We must never forget that the Spirit is not only lowly water, he is also the wind – the breath – of God. He is that holy hurricane which we can neither predict nor control. We may know that he is God's power in *action*, but we must recognize this means that he will often introduce surprising new developments.

Ever since Pentecost, the Holy Spirit has been changing believers' ideas and attitudes. In every century, he's been busy shaking the church's traditions, questioning its values, and pressing it to break new ground in evangelistic mission and social action.

The smallest glance at the last two thousand years of church history should be enough to convince us that the

The Spirit shakes the church's traditions, questions its values, and presses it to break new ground in mission

Age of the Spirit is an era of almost constant change.

The book of Acts lists some major changes brought by the Spirit: the amazing events of Pentecost, Peter's struggle to enter Cornelius' house, Paul's pioneering journeys. Paul's letters show how the Spirit of truth changed Jewish believers' ideas about Gentiles, circumcision, faith and grace. And so through the centuries – right up to today – the church has struggled to keep in step with the Spirit, as he goes on urging us to accept new ways of showing God's love and to embrace fresh structures which are more relevant to our culture.

The Spirit Today

We live in incredibly exciting times. During the twentieth century, the wind of God seems to have been blowing with exceptional strength and power, bringing truth, life and power to the church – and pointing tens of millions of people to Jesus Christ.

Although spiritual gifts can be seen in every century since Pentecost, the last hundred years have been the clearest fulfillment of Joel's prophecy so far!

Pentecostal revival

In the first decade of the twentieth century, there was a spectacular outpouring of the Holy Spirit which brought Pentecostal-type churches into being. These churches have now spread right around the world and have become by far the fastest growing section of the global church – especially in South America, Africa and Asia.

In the first half of this century, God used 'pentecostal revival' to remind ordinary believers that spiritual gifts were still for everyone, that miracles were still part of God's purposes for today, and that every believer had a vital part to play in God's plan of mission.

Through this revival, the Spirit of truth restored the experience of being filled with the Holy Spirit into the everyday expectation and thinking of millions of believers.

The early pentecostal movement mainly affected ordinary working people, and had little impact on traditional clergy and denominational churches. It was a Spirit-led movement which grew through dynamic witnessing and delightful worship.

Charismatic renewal

During the last thirty years, there has been another, similar, outpouring of God's Spirit. Charismatic renewal has affected many parts of the world-wide church which had not been touched by pentecostal revival.

The Spirit has brought fresh life, new forms of worship and spiritual gifts back to tens of thousands of traditional denominational churches. A general acceptance has grown of the reality of miracles and the need to be filled or anointed with the Spirit.

The renewing presence of the Spirit can be seen in all sorts of small ways. Sermons and services have increased in length, books and conferences have proliferated, and

> Unspeakable joy has replaced sober reverence as the dominant emotion of charismatic and pentecostal Christians

new churches have started as people have been filled with a desire for good teaching.

Offerings have mushroomed as believers have wanted to give to all sorts of needs. Prayer has become more of a dynamic reality. Intercession is increasingly important. Thanksgiving is a delight rather than a routine chore. Unspeakable joy has replaced sober reverence as the dominant emotion of charismatic and pentecostal Christians.

Third world church growth

One of the great acts of the Spirit in the last twenty years has been largely unseen in North America and Europe.

The church has grown at a fantastic rate across the 'Third World' – in South and Central America, South East Asia, and all of Africa except the northern Muslim countries. Missionaries had been going to the Third World for a hundred years from North America and Western Europe. Much outstanding pioneer evangelism had been done. But in the last thirty years, the church in these nations has started to grow very rapidly – at a much faster rate than the population.

This growth has mainly been in churches which – through the influence of pentecostalism and charismatic renewal – are open to the influence of the Holy Spirit and are not dependent on Western missionaries.

Every member ministry

The principle of every member being actively involved in ministry is one of the key themes which have been highlighted by the Spirit of truth in the last two decades.

Thirty years ago, virtually every part of the church believed that nearly all aspects of ministry were reserved for full-time, fully paid, male ministers.

Today, it is generally recognized that every member – whatever their age, sex or education – has a vital and unique part to play in the church.

> Every member – whatever their age, sex or education – has a vital and unique part to play in the church

The Spirit has shown us the importance of leadership teams, of training and equipping all members in ministry, of recognizing special ministries in lay people, and of appreciating the significance of Paul's teaching about the interdependence of *every* part of the body.

We have had to face the fact that the Holy Spirit gives his gifts to all believers, not just to a special few, and that our church structures should reflect this spiritual reality.

Signs and wonders

Except in groups affected by pentecostal revival, most of this century's evangelism has revolved around preaching. Only very recently has this been changed by the Spirit.

Suddenly, the Holy Spirit has helped Western churches to understand that he wants to support our evangelism with signs and wonders – with miracles of healing, deliverance, provision and restoration.

The Spirit of truth has helped us to grasp the fact that words about Christ are not enough to convince unbelieving people. They need to see God's power in action. The Holy Spirit has highlighted our need for power – and has shown us the truth that this power is always available in him.

So 'power' evangelism, 'power' healing and all sorts of 'power' ministries have recently developed right round

> Words about Christ are not enough, unbelieving people need to see God's power in action

the world. These should stand alongside the witness to Christ of our words and our lives.

Spiritual gifts

In the last twenty years, the spiritual gifts mentioned in the New Testament have been more widely talked about than at any time since the first century.

As Christian people have begun to appreciate the person and ministry of the Holy Spirit, so they have started to accept and discuss his gifts. Vast numbers of books, sermons and conferences have focused on matters like prophecy, tongues, discernment, words of knowledge and wisdom, special faith, miracles and healing.

The place and function of apostles, prophets, evangelists, pastors and teachers has been better understood – and these gifts have begun to equip many saints for ministry in their local areas.

Today – as never before – the church knows about spiritual gifts. Yet, sadly, they are more often talked about than used in witness and worship. Many believers have thought them to be rewards for supposed spirituality and have used them to suggest a form of spiritual elitism.

The truth is that the Spirit's gifts are given to help *every* believer get their God-appointed job done in the power of the Spirit. They are given so that we can extend the church and establish God's kingdom.

Holy lifestyle

There has been much talk about the power of the Spirit this century, especially in the last ten years. There has not been the same emphasis on the purity of the *Holy* Spirit.

Throughout history the church has swung between these two aspects of the Spirit, and only rarely – as in early monasticism and early pentecostalism – has it embraced both at the same time.

Many Christians today live holy, blameless lives with no noticeable power, and there are others who have power but a carnal divisive nature. The Holy Spirit is perfectly pure and infinitely powerful. If we are filled with him – with the very presence of God – we should surely share both his charisma *and* his character.

The rest of this book is given over to showing how both these elements can be held in balance within the church today. For the truth is that our world desperately needs Christians who so live in the Spirit's presence that every aspect of their lives points people to the living Lord Jesus.

PART TWO

JESUS AND THE HOLY SPIRIT

Jesus shows us what God is like. When we look at him, we can see the nature and character of God. Everything that Jesus says and does reveals something about God.

But Jesus is also the Perfect Man. When we look at him, we can see what we are meant to be like. All his words and actions show how men and women should live.

When Jesus came from heaven, he did not leave his divinity behind. He could have given commands and made miracles happen like God. Instead, Jesus chose to depend on the Holy Spirit. He chose to live and minister by relying entirely on the initiative and power of the Holy Spirit.

This means that, as we read the Gospels, we can see the perfect example of the ministry that God has for us.

Of course, there are some differences. Jesus was able to experience the Spirit without measure so there are aspects of his life and ministry which we can never match. But our lives are meant to reflect Jesus' ministry. It is vitally important we realize that – ultimately – there is only one ministry: Jesus'. We either share his ministry, or we struggle along on our own.

THE ANOINTED ONE

Throughout the world, Jesus is known by the title *Christ*. This comes from the Greek word *Christos*, which means 'anointed' and is exactly the same as the Hebrew word *Messiah*. He is 'the Anointed One'.

Jesus claimed to be anointed in Luke 4:18-21; and Peter recognized Jesus as the Christ, the Anointed, in Mark 8:29 and Acts 10:38. It is clear from these verses that the anointing is the Holy Spirit and that it is for service.

> Anointing consecrates us to God, dedicates us for service, and then equips us with power for service

In the Old Testament, prophets, priests, kings and holy objects were anointed with holy oil as an act of consecration to God and in dedication for serving God.

In the New Testament, the symbolic anointing with oil was transformed into the reality of anointing with Holy Spirit. The anointing still consecrates the person to God and dedicates them for service, but then it goes much further. It actually equips them with the power that they need to perform their God-given task of service.

The moment of Jesus' anointing

Jesus did not become 'The Christ' when the Spirit anointed him at his baptism, for he always had been the Christ. Rather, the anointing openly declared who he was – in the same way that the Father's words at the baptism revealed him as the Son.

More importantly for us, Jesus' anointing consecrated and equipped him to serve as 'The Christ'. We have already seen that Jesus' earthly life was lived in the Spirit even from before he was born. Matthew 1:18-21 and Luke 1:31-35 show that he was conceived by the Spirit.

Jesus, born of the Spirit, lived as a carpenter for about thirty years. But before he could begin his ministry he needed to be anointed with the Spirit.

For his first thirty years, Jesus had a holy, sinless lifestyle, but – with rare exception – nobody noticed any power or authority. That changed when he was anointed with the Spirit at his baptism.

Jesus' baptism was his commissioning and equipping for service. It was his moment of visible, public consecration to God's work.

> Jesus became the bearer of the Spirit so that he might become the baptizer in the Spirit

Jesus walked into the river and left behind his family, job, security and possessions. He put himself unconditionally at the disposal of the Father. He was baptized in dependence on God to reveal the next step in his life.

As Jesus came out of the river, the Spirit came down, down like a dove, and rested on him. John 1:32-34 testifies, 'I saw the Spirit descending from heaven like a dove, and he remained upon him'.

Matthew 3:13-17, Mark1:9-11, Luke 3:21-22 also

describe Jesus' anointing with the Spirit. In that moment, Jesus became the bearer of the Spirit so that he might become the baptizer in the Spirit.

The effects of Jesus' anointing

John 3:34 shows that Jesus' anointing was completely without measure. So he has became known as Jesus Christ – Jesus the Anointed. From his anointing onwards, people were amazed by Jesus' power: he was 'not as other men'.

Matthew 4:1 and Mark 1:12 show that the first consequence for Jesus of his anointing was to be driven by the Spirit into the desert to do battle with the devil. His anointing meant that he had to face terrible temptations.

Luke 4:1 portrays Jesus as 'filled with the Holy Spirit' when he entered the wilderness. After his triumphant struggle with Satan, Luke describes Jesus in 4:14 as returning to Galilee 'in the power of the Spirit'.

We've already seen the contrast in Jesus' life between being filled with the Spirit and being filled with the power of the Spirit. To be filled with the Spirit is the first step. The power only comes when our fullness has been tested, when we have obeyed God during evil temptations.

> **The power only comes when our fullness has been tested, when we have obeyed God during evil temptations**

Luke 4:16-27 shows that Jesus went directly to Nazareth from the desert. He read from Isaiah 61 and applied it to himself. He claimed that the Spirit was upon him because he had been anointed. Now he had the anointing – the help of the Spirit – to preach, to heal, to bring freedom.

Acts 10:38 shows that, through the anointing, 'God was with' Jesus. In the Spirit, he could now do as a man what before he had been unable to do in his humanity. He could heal 'all who were oppressed by the devil'.

We know that Jesus' life was lived fully in the Spirit. The Spirit gave him his power and emotions. He filled Jesus with joy. He helped him to drive out demons and teach. He even gave Jesus the strength to sacrifice himself on the cross.

Everything about Jesus' life – his character, his words, his deeds – was the direct consequence of being born of the Spirit and being anointed with the Spirit.

THE MODEL MINISTRY

If Jesus needed the anointing of the Spirit for his ministry on earth, how much more must we need the same anointing to reach people with the Good News of God's love!

We should thank God that exactly the same Holy Spirit anointing which rested on Jesus is promised to us.

In Acts 1:8 Jesus states that, 'you shall receive power when the Holy Spirit has come upon you; and you shall be witnesses to me'. In Romans 8:11, Paul tells us that the same Spirit who raised Jesus from the dead lives in us.

Jesus was anointed to do the things listed in Isaiah 61:1-2 and Luke 4:18-19. Exactly the same work still needs to be done today, and the same anointing is available to us all.

We know that Jesus is our example in all things. We are called to obey the Father as Jesus obeyed the Father. We are meant to depend on the Spirit as Jesus depended on the Spirit. We are meant to love and serve the people around us as Jesus did – and so on.

> We should thank God that exactly the same Holy Spirit anointing which rested on Jesus is promised to us

But more than that, we are meant to share Jesus' ministry. We know that the church is Christ's body on earth – his hands and legs while he reigns in heaven. This must mean that we follow the pattern of his ministry rather than our own inclination or ideas!

Christ's ministry is the model for all ministry. If we want to minister in the power of the Spirit, we should look at Jesus. He is the great Servant Minister who perfectly ministered in the power and full demonstration of the Spirit.

The mighty king

Jesus' ministry seems to have had several great themes or purposes. Firstly, he came to break the power of evil and death. The fallen angel Lucifer had taken authority on earth and the whole world was under his sway.

In his ministry, in the power of the Spirit, Jesus established the kingdom of heaven and disarmed the evil powers of darkness. He preached a gospel of repentance, taught his followers about judgment and the consequence of disobedience. He gave them clear guidelines for behaviour.

Jesus broke the power of evil and death

In short, the Gospels show us that Jesus was a mighty king who was concerned to found a kingdom. He ruled over nature. He ruled over disease. He ruled over demons. Lepers were healed. The dead were revived. Devils feared. Storms obeyed. But God's people of Israel would not receive their king.

There are only two ways to respond to the king: with obedience or rejection. Jesus still calls people, 'Follow me'. Some obey without question. Many reject him. Others try to negotiate easier conditions.

If Jesus is our model ministry, it means that something of his kingly power and authority should be seen in us. We will confront evil powers. We will be face to face with disease. We will preach a message of repentance, judgment and obedience. We will remind people of Jesus' clear commands and the kingdom behaviour that he expects.

But, remember, we will only be able to share his royal effectiveness when we share his Holy Spirit anointing! We will only be able to be his feet and hands on earth when we are filled and empowered with the Holy Spirit as he was.

The suffering servant

A second great theme of Jesus' ministry was to seek and to save the lost. Jesus came to save lost, needy people who were powerless to save themselves.

At great personal sacrifice, he came to make atonement for the sins of humanity, to act as a substitute for every man, woman and child, and to bear God's wrath against sin.

Through his life and ministry, Jesus showed himself to be the suffering servant of God who comes to serve and to offer himself as a sacrifice.

Jesus was at the beck and call of the crowds. He responded to needs immediately. He worked unobtrusively and asked people to tell nobody about their miracle. He served unseen and was ready to serve unthanked.

> Jesus came to serve and to offer himself as a sacrifice

Jesus' motive for ministry was compassion and love. His life was full of prayer. He made it clear that he had come 'not to be served but to serve, and to give his life as a ransom for many' (Mark 10:45). He called others not only to follow him but also 'to take up the cross' (Mark 10:21).

The whole of Jesus' earthly ministry was coloured by the cross. It is impossible for us to separate Jesus' signs and wonders ministry from his supreme sacrifice, from the absolute suffering and terrible rejection that he endured.

All this means that, when we model our lives and ministries on Christ, we will willingly embrace service, sacrifice and suffering. Passages like Philippians 2:5-8 will come alive when we realize that we follow God's humble suffering servant.

Some believers who have grasped the truth about 'power ministry' have sadly forgotten that the anointing for power is the humble, gentle, self-effacing Holy Spirit. We should not seek for power and kingly authority unless we are prepared to embrace lowly service and Christ-like suffering.

The perfect human being

Another theme or purpose of Christ's anointed life and ministry was to demonstrate a life of perfect consecration to the Father. He came to be the example for men and women of all ages and every race.

Jesus was not just a king and a servant, he was also the ideal human being, the perfect specimen of humanity, the pattern life for all humankind. In his daily death to self he showed us how we should live.

In his ministry, Jesus was tested in every possible way, he was subject to ordinary conflict and emotions, yet he remained without sin.

The gospels show that Jesus is the sympathetic friend of sinners and a man to be followed. He was an ordinary, poor man who was on the side of the lowest members of society. He taught more about money than any subject other than the kingdom –

> In his daily death to self, Jesus showed us how we should live and die

and constantly warned about the dangers of wealth and demanded extreme generosity in his followers.

He pressed home the need for forgiveness, urging people to forgive others and practising this himself on the cross.

This shows that our everyday lives really matter. We cannot separate ministry from morals. Jesus' power and purity were equal evidences of his anointing. If we model ourselves on Christ we will live with his holiness – as well as healing with his authority and serving with his compassion.

The holy God

A fourth main purpose of Jesus' ministry was to show what God is like. He came to reveal the glorious Father. He came as God's living Word – as a unique and complete revelation of the invisible God – to reproduce the divine nature in humankind.

Jesus is not only the royal son of David, the suffering servant of God, the perfect example of humanity, he is also the glorious Son of God.

Jesus came to reveal the glorious Father

Jesus' ministry orders us to obey the king; it invites us to allow the servant to serve us; it asks us to follow the perfect man. But it also dazzles us with life, light, love, truth and glory so that we will love and believe in God's glorious, light-bearing, life-bringing Son.

Everywhere he went, in everything he said and did, he revealed the presence of God. Jesus emphasized his oneness with the Father and explained that his words and deeds were the very words and deeds of the Father. When people looked and listened to Jesus, they saw and heard the living God.

So too our lives and ministries are meant to point people

to the Father. The Spirit is God, and when we are filled with the Spirit – when we are in him and he is in us – we will radiate the presence of God in all his power and purity.

It is a great tragedy that the church has seldom embraced all the different themes of Jesus' ministry in balance. Some sections have tended to major on the kingly theme, whilst others have focused on the serving

> **When we are filled with the Spirit we will radiate the presence of God in all his power and purity**

or human or divine themes. Yet when we depend entirely on the Spirit we will surely reveal all these emphases – just as Jesus did.

Involved others

Jesus spent about three years in earthly ministry. He used this time to train the disciples in ministry so that they could carry on his work after he returned to heaven.

There was an inner group of twelve apostles who travelled with Jesus, living with him, listening to him, watching him and being deeply involved with his ministry.

Matthew 10, Mark 6:7-13 and Luke 9:1-6 describe how these twelve men were sent out in pairs to live and minister in the same way as Jesus. Please read these passages and see how Jesus instructed them both in how they should minister and in how they should behave.

Luke 10:1-23 reports that at least another 72 people – and these might have included women – were also sent out to live and minister in pairs. Please read their instructions and see how they were instructed to live simply as well as to preach and heal the sick.

Finally, just before his ascension, Jesus told all the disciples to 'Go, therefore and make disciples of all nations, baptizing them in the name of the Father and of the Son and of the Holy Spirit, teaching them to observe all things that I have commanded you; and lo, I am with you always, even to the end of the age' (Matthew 28:19-20).

This commission was entrusted not just to the generation of that day, but to all generations – to us. We are to observe everything that Jesus has commanded. We cannot pick and choose which words we obey. We have to live with his purity *and* minister with his power.

By now we should know that we can do this only if we share Jesus' anointing. We need to live as he did in the presence of the Spirit, depending completely on the Holy Spirit for strength and guidance.

Jesus wants to involve us in his ministry. This is an amazing privilege and an enormous responsibility. He has chosen us to be his feet and hands, to be his voice, so that he can work through us today.

> Jesus has chosen us to be his feet and hands, to be his voice, so that he can work through us today

Every believer reading these words has been personally picked by God to be part of Christ's body on earth. He wants to carry out Jesus' ministry through me and through you. He wants to do today what we read about in the gospels – and he wants to involve us in this ministry. It is almost too wonderful to bear!

THE BAPTIZER

We've seen that anyone who turns to the Gospels to learn about Jesus is faced with John's announcement that Jesus 'will baptize you with Holy Spirit and fire'.

Whichever gospel we read, this is one of the first facts we learn about Jesus. As far as John the Baptist seems to have been concerned, the most important aspect of Jesus' ministry was that he would be the Baptizer.

The disciples were people who had been sent out by Jesus in ministry. They had preached and seen God work wonderful miracles through them. Yet Jesus told them, in Acts 1:1-11, that they had to wait until they received the power of the Spirit when they were baptized by him with the Holy Spirit.

Their years with Jesus were not enough. Their ministry experience was inadequate. They needed Jesus to baptize them in the Holy Spirit.

> The word *baptism* points to an unrepeatable experience of initiation. It is not an end in itself but the doorway to a new way of living

Sadly, there has been some division in the church about this wonderful experience. Much of the confusion seems to have been due to misunderstandings about terminology.

The New Testament contains five phrases which all describe the same powerful encounter with the Holy Spirit. Each phrase sheds some light on a different aspect of this wonderful experience. We need to appreciate them all if we are to understand what Jesus seeks to accomplish by his gracious gift.

Baptized in the Holy Spirit

This phrase occurs six times in the New Testament. Matthew 3:11, Mark 1:8, Luke 3:16, John 1:33, Acts 1:5 & Acts 11:16 refer to the baptism which John promised that the Messiah – the Anointed One – would bring.

The word *baptism* points to an unrepeatable experience of initiation. It is not an end in itself but the doorway to a new way of living. When Jesus baptized the church in the Spirit at Pentecost, it was the moment of initiation into the Holy Spirit's brand new age.

But Pentecost was also a day of first fruits. It looked forward to a far greater harvest. Each succeeding Christian can enter into the benefits of Pentecost. We can join them in the baptistry of the Holy Spirit to receive this baptism from the very hands of Jesus.

Filled with the Holy Spirit

This phrase is used twelve times in the New Testament. Luke uses it to describe what happened to people both before and after Pentecost. He also uses it to describe both the process of becoming filled as well as the ongoing state of being filled.

We have seen this phrase suggests that we are not 'cups' who contain the Spirit, but 'sponges' who are filled by being plunged into the Spirit. This should help us to see that becoming filled and being baptized are one and the same experience.

> We are filled with the Spirit because we are immersed in the Spirit and are saturated by the Spirit

We are filled with the Spirit because we are immersed in the Spirit and are saturated by the Spirit. From the moment of initiation we remain full, as long as we stay – by obedience – in the baptistry. This means that we continue to be filled with the Spirit while we go on living in the Holy Spirit.

Many people know that Ephesians 5:18 is best translated as 'go on being filled with the Spirit'. This does not mean asking God to fill us again and again – to top us up like a half-empty cup! It means continuing in the state of fullness which was started by Christ when he immersed us in the Holy Spirit.

Anointed with the Spirit

Like baptism, 'anointing' is a word which is best used to describe a new beginning. It shows that our experience of the Spirit should launch us into something fresh – a new depth of service or dimension of living that we have not known before.

We have seen that prophets, priests and kings were anointed with oil in the Old Testament – once, at the start of their ministries – as an act of consecration to God. And we know that Jesus claimed to be the *Christos* – the Anointed.

2 Corinthians 1:21 and 1 John 2:20,27 describe Christians as people who have been anointed by Jesus with the Holy Spirit. This phrase suggests a once-for-all experience of consecration to God and dedication for service.

The concept of anointing is implied in the many New Testament passages which speak of the Spirit falling upon, resting upon, coming down upon, and being poured out.

Sealed with the Spirit

This expression is used in 2 Corinthians 1:22, Ephesians 1:13 & 4:30. The normal legal meaning of a seal is plain. It is added after the signature as a guarantee of authenticity. When we become Christians, the legal documentation of eternal life is given. God's signature can be seen. But it is all too good to believe. There must be some mistake. Then the seal is stamped upon us

The seal is stamped upon us to provide authentic, believable, experiential proof of our inheritance in Christ

to provide authentic, believable, experiential proof of our inheritance in Christ.

John 6:26-27 shows that Jesus is one upon whom the seal has been placed. This must refer to the gift of the Spirit at his baptism. So too the coming down of the Spirit upon the church at Pentecost was like a seal. It assured the believers that Jesus' promises were genuine.

Received the Spirit

This phrase is used twice, in Acts 8:14-17 and Acts 19:2-7. Some people argue that we can only receive the Spirit when we become a Christian – when we believe. These passages show that this idea is not credible.

These Samaritans and Ephesians are clearly identified as 'believers'. They were people who already were genuine disciples. But they had not received the Spirit in the way that the New Testament expected.

It does not matter much which of these biblical expressions we use to describe our power encounter with the Spirit. What matters is that we are saturated by the Spirit so that his holy life and dynamic power can control us.

Distinct experience

Conversion is a process not an instantaneous happening. It includes being born again, repentance, faith, forgiveness of sins, baptism in water and receiving the Holy Spirit.

It can be condensed into a few minutes, with all the aspects occurring nearly simultaneously. Or it can be spread over a lifetime – though God does not want it to take that long!

We know of some people who have been born again at some point in their life, but who have not been baptized, or gone on in repentance, or received the Holy Spirit. We can

Preaching which emphasizes or neglects any part of conversion leads to inadequately equipped Christians

think of people who are powerful but carnal leaders, and others who are holy but spiritually weak. It seems to me that preaching which emphasizes or neglects any part of conversion must lead to inadequately equipped Christians.

In John 3, Jesus distinguished between seeing the kingdom and entering the kingdom. God gives the gift of spiritual sight when we are born again by the Spirit. This is when our eternal destiny changes: we start to see things 'God's way' and begin to develop a desire for spiritual matters.

However, it is God's will for us not only to be able to see his kingdom but also to enter deeply into it. This is what creates the possibility of victory over sin, of power in witness, and of growth into the likeness of Christ.

Nobody disagrees that being born again is the work of

It is possible to be a believer and not be baptized in the Spirit

the Holy Spirit. It is not possible to become a Christian apart from the work of the Spirit. John 3:1-8, Romans 8:1-14 & 1 Corinthians 2:10-14 make this plain.

We cannot choose to be born again, and we cannot make it happen. We do not know when it will occur, and we may be unaware or confused when it is taking place. We just know when it has happened for we find ourselves believing what we could never believe before. All this is accomplished *by* the Spirit. It is his work.

However, it is possible to be a believer and not be baptized in the Spirit. This is a distinct experience which is additional to belief and is accomplished *by* Jesus. He is the baptizer. The Holy Spirit is the element.

Most Old Testament saints were believers who were not anointed with the Spirit. The apostles were born again, miracle-working believers, but they were not baptized in the Spirit until Pentecost.

The 3,000 devout Jews of Acts 2 were born again by the Spirit as Peter spoke. This was unconditional. But their receiving of the Spirit depended on their repentance, belief and baptism. The Samaritans of Acts 8 had already been born again and baptized in water, but they did not receive the Spirit until the apostles laid hands on them.

Saul, in Acts 9, was born again on the Damascus road. Ananias did not need to preach the Gospel, only lay hands for healing and the filling with the Spirit.

Acts 10:4 shows that Cornelius and his household had been accepted by God before Peter arrived and before they received the Spirit.

The Ephesian disciples of Acts 19 are most striking. Surely there must have been something about them which caused Paul to ask them whether or not they had received the Holy Spirit when they became believers. This makes it obvious that Paul thought it possible to believe and not to receive the Spirit.

> It is not a case of first and second blessings, nor of superior and inferior Christians, but of total or partial conversion

Ephesians 1:13 is another clinching verse which shows that receiving the Holy Spirit is separate and subsequent to believing in Jesus. The period of time between the two experiences is not important, it is the distinction between them which is critical to understand.

Please appreciate that this is not a case of first and second blessings, nor of superior and inferior Christians, but of total or partial conversion.

Regeneration – being born again – is enacted by the Holy Spirit. This changes our destiny and begins the process of conversion. Our anointing with the Spirit by Jesus may then be a moment later or half a lifetime away. But when it happens we start to live in the Spirit and can begin to serve God more powerfully and reveal his presence more clearly.

JESUS' EARTHLY MINISTRY

We know that, after his anointing, Jesus spent almost three years preaching, teaching and healing. Quite simply, he was the greatest teacher there has ever been and the mightiest miracle worker that there ever will be.

We have seen that Jesus offers us the same anointing as he had – though not in the same measure – that he calls us to carry out the same work he did, and that his balanced ministry is the perfect model for us today. However we must also grasp and apply four deep principles which undergirded Jesus' earthly ministry if we are going to 'follow' him closely.

With prayer

Jesus was a man of prayer. He rose early to pray and remained awake late to pray. We can see him in prayer at every stage of his ministry.

He prayed at his baptism, Luke 3:21, and after much ministry, Mark 1:35, 6:46, Luke 5:16. He prayed for a complete night before selecting the inner group of twelve disciples, Luke 6:12. He prayed when revealing himself as the Anointed One of God, Luke 9:18.

Sometimes he prayed alone in the presence of his disciples – as at his Transfiguration, Luke 9:28-29. He prayed at the last supper, John 17, and in Gethsemane, Luke 22:41,

Mark 14:32. He even prayed at the crucifixion, Luke 23:34, and after his resurrection, Luke 24:30.

Prayer was one of the secrets of Jesus' dynamic ministry. If we want to follow him, intercessory prayer will dominate our ministries too.

With obedience

John 5:19, 30; 6:38; 7:28-29; 8:26, 28-29; 10:18 & 12:49-50 are an extraordinary series of sayings. Jesus, the perfect man, the great healer, the mighty deliverer, the wonder counsellor, was the one who stated time and again that he himself could do nothing.

How many of us today think that about ourselves? How many leaders long to be able to say it about their ministry?

But Jesus, by a massive effort of self-denial, restricted himself to saying, doing and going what and where the Father told him. Acts 2:22 makes it clear that it was God who performed the miracles *through* Jesus.

We know that we are meant to obey God. The

> Jesus never did anything on his own initiative. He only did those few things that the Father told him

devil tempts us to do the opposite – either to *disobey* God's command or to *presume* to do something that he has not commanded. Both actions are equally sinful – and Jesus never disobeyed God and he never acted or spoke without first knowing God's prompting.

In the temptations, Jesus was urged to presume – to act independently of God – to work a miracle without any instructions; to move from a natural desire for food, power and prestige to a sinful presumption to satisfy those desires.

Jesus was not tempted to perform evil deeds, but to do his own deeds. However, Jesus never did anything on his

71

own initiative: he only did the things that the Father told him.

Luke 22:39-46 tells the story of the supreme moment of temptation in Jesus' ministry: a struggle not with Satan but with God. The issue was simple, whose will would be done.

Verse 42 must be one of the most important moments in history. Jesus submitted to God's will with these words, 'Nevertheless, not my will, but yours, be done'.

We will begin to share Jesus' ministry only when we obey like this in the face of an equally hard personal struggle.

With compassion

Sometimes we so concentrate on the miracles God worked through Jesus that we miss the motive behind the miracles.

Jesus did not minister to attract attention to himself, he ministered because he loved the needy people and cared about their needs. Holy compassion drove Jesus to give needy people his time, his love, his energy, his life – his all.

Mark 1:41 records Jesus' compassion for one leper. Mark 6:34 reveals his compassion for a vast crowd of needy people. And Mark 10:21 describes Jesus' feelings towards the wealthy aristocrat who would not become a follower. 'Then Jesus, looking at him, loved him.'

With the Spirit's help

We have already seen that Jesus' anointing with the Spirit and submission to the Father made all the difference.

Passages like John 5:19 and John 14:10 show us that Jesus restricted himself to saying and doing what the Father instructed. When Jesus moved with the Father – when he lived in the Spirit's presence – the anointing enabled and empowered whatever needed to be done.

Jesus' ministry was based entirely on his relationship

with the Father and the Spirit. He only did what the Father was doing – and the Spirit helped him to carry that out. It's exactly the same for us!

However, Jesus did not minister only through the anointing of the Spirit and according to the Father's will, he also ministered through the gifts that the Spirit gave him – precisely the same ones that the Spirit gives us today!

Power and anointing are words we use to describe the general help of the Spirit.

Particular gifts describe specific help that the Spirit gives at special moments for distinctive purposes.

> Jesus did not depend on a pattern or formula when he was ministering, he depended on the help of the Spirit

Jesus had tremendous skill in ministering according to the gifts of the Spirit. In fact we see all the New Testament gifts in Jesus' ministry except tongues and interpretation.

For example, we can see Jesus using the gift of faith in Mark 11:20-25 & John 11:41-42. We can see the gift of miracles in Mark 6:30-52 & John 2:1-11; the gift of healing in Matthew 4:23-25 & Mark 5:21-43; the word of wisdom in Luke 13:10-17; the discerning of spirits in Matthew 16:17-23; the gift of prophecy in John 2:19; and the word of knowledge in John 1:47-50 & John 4:16-20.

It is very important we grasp the truth that Jesus did not depend on a pattern or formula when he was ministering – he depended on the help and prompting of the Spirit.

When we read the gospels we see that Jesus ministered differently on almost every occasion. Sometimes he touched people sometimes he did not. Sometimes he spoke commands to bring healing or drive out demons, sometimes he did not. Sometimes he made the person do something. Sometimes he did not.

Jesus never ministered according to his experience. Instead, he always ministered by obeying the Father and depending on the Spirit – and that usually meant something different for each person he helped.

Too often today we think that because something worked for one person we will do the same thing for someone else with a similar problem. That is relying on our experience rather than depending on the Spirit. If we are followers of Jesus, we will rely on the Spirit's guidance, power and gifts.

JESUS' MINISTRY TODAY

One of the most wonderful truths we can grasp about Jesus is the fact that his ministry did not end at the cross. The stories we read in the gospels record the start of Jesus' ministry – not the sum total of his ministry.

Matthew 28:18-20, Mark 16:15-18 and Luke 24:44-49 describe Jesus' charge to his disciples to continue his ministry – and his promise to carry on working with them.

The book of Acts shows how Jesus worked through the first Christians – through the church. Please read this selection of verses and see how Jesus' ministry develops: Acts 3:6; 5:12-16; 8:4-8; 9:32-43 & 16:6-10.

We can see that all kinds of signs and wonders and healings were performed through the apostles with many people turning to Jesus. Leaders were guided by the Spirit to go to specific places to preach the good news. The gospel was preached everywhere, and was confirmed by many miracles – even by people being raised from the dead.

And so Jesus has carried on ministering to the needy people of our world right down through the centuries. He began the work. Saints through the ages have been Christ's body on earth, doing his work. It is now our responsibility to continue exactly the same work that we read about in the New Testament.

But please remember, Jesus ministry is the *only*

> It is now our responsibility to continue exactly the same work that we read about in the New Testament

ministry. The ministry belongs to him. It is *his* work that we are called to do as *his* body, in the same way that Jesus was called to do the Father's work. This means that – because it is Jesus' work we are doing – we do *not* have a ministry of our own: it is his and his alone.

He prays for us

We have seen that prayer was one of the secrets of Jesus' dynamic ministry. It still is!

Romans 8:34 states that, 'It is Christ who died, and furthermore is also risen, who is even at the right hand of God, who also makes intercession for us'.

Hebrews 7:25 reminds us that Jesus, 'is able to save to the uttermost those who come to God through him, since he ever lives to make intercession for them'.

These two verses reveal the present heavenly ministry of Jesus. Right now, he is praying for me and for you. When we are tempted, he is praying for us. When we are prompted to speak to a person, he is praying for us. While we are ministering, he is praying for us!

Wherever we are, whatever we are doing, Jesus Christ is at the right hand of the Father praying for us to carry out his ministry in the manner that he expects!

He provides the resources

We know that Jesus has not left us empty-handed in the face of an overwhelmingly strong enemy. He has disarmed and defeated the forces of darkness, and given us a measure of the same anointing that he had to carry out his works.

But Ephesians 4:11-12 shows us that Jesus has done even more. He has given gifts 'for the equipping of the saints for the work of ministry'.

These gifts are leadership roles in the church. It is sad that many local congregations have read this particular scripture for so long and yet have expected their minister to fulfil all the leadership roles and do all the ministry himself.

It is even sadder that some church leaders have studied the verse and ignored its implications for their situation. These important gifts have been given to the church by Jesus so that *every* member can begin to minister.

Apostles (the word means *one who is sent*) are usually pioneers who spearhead the work of the gospel. They demonstrate God's presence by their actions, establish new Christian communities, and create many opportunities for believers to minister.

> **These important gifts have been given to the church by Jesus so that *every* member can begin to minister**

Prophets encourage believers by explaining what God is doing, and by challenging the standards and behaviour of the world and the church. Ideally, they pass on only what God is thinking and do not taint the message with their own opinions and cultural values.

Evangelists are leaders who enable ordinary believers to live the dedicated life of God and gossip the Good News in language which the people around them understand. They help the saints to reach out in witness, they don't do it for them!

Pastors and teachers build on the foundations laid by the other three leaders. They stay in one place, often for many years, caring for the church, teaching it the word of God and the ways of Jesus, and helping the people to minister and develop God's kingdom in their locality.

Although we may have been given the Spirit, we can't get the job done on our own. We need each other and we need these Jesus-sent godly leaders to train and encourage us.

He works with us

Sometimes the work of ministry and the pressures of life can get us down. So we should never stop reminding ourselves and each other of the glorious truth that we are never alone. Jesus is with us by the Spirit.

He promised to be with us in Matthew 28:20 – to the end of time. Mark 16:20 points out that the promise has been kept. 'They went out and preached everywhere, the Lord working with them and confirming the word through the accompanying signs.'

That is a basic principle of Christian ministry. We are the legs and mouth of Jesus in the world today. We go and speak – when and where he leads. He confirms our words by special signs. We do not have to worry about miracles, we cannot perform miracles. But Jesus, by the Spirit, works with us and confirms our words – when they are his words!

He works through the church

One of the themes which the Spirit of truth has recently been reminding us about is the importance of our relationship with other believers.

When a person is born again by the Spirit, a new relationship starts not only with God but also with all other Christians in the church.

In Ephesians 2:15-16 Paul shows that, through Jesus' death, God created one single New Man, and that we all have been reconciled to God 'in one Body'. This means that, though we do all have a personal relationship with God, we are also united with each other.

Jesus' ministry on earth continues through both individual believers and also through the united body – the New Man – the church. Jesus' John 17:20-26 prayer shows how vital our united relationships are in enabling the world to believe in him.

Unity is one of those vital facts which gives our evangelism credibility. How can we expect the world to listen to our message of reconciliation and forgiveness when churches are divided or competitive?

> Jesus' John 17:20-26 prayer shows how important united relationships are in enabling the world to believe in him

The New Testament uses a variety of word pictures to describe the united church. Each picture provides us with an insight into an aspect of Jesus' continuing ministry on earth through the church.

In 1 Peter 2:9 describes us as a 'chosen generation, a royal priesthood, a holy nation, his own special people, that you may proclaim the praises of him who called you out of darkness into his marvellous light; who once were not a people but are now the people of God'.

Peter's descriptions express similar ideas to Paul's terms for united disciples – a bride, 2 Corinthians 11:2, a holy temple, 1 Corinthians 3:16, a body, Ephesians 1:23, and the church, 1 Corinthians 1:2.

We have been carefully chosen to be *the bride of Jesus*. This means that we are loved with an eternal love and will share Jesus' inheritance of all things.

We are *the royal priesthood* who serve the king by sacrificially serving the king's people in all sorts of ways, and by filling ourselves – the holy temple or dwelling place of God – with the priestly sacrifices of prayer and praise. Surely it should be a tremendously high honour to serve the ultimate royal family in their royal residence.

We are a holy nation, and have been set apart for a corporate life of dedication and consecration. We form *the body of Christ* so that he can carry on living his perfect life on earth through us.

We deeply belong to God. We are *his church* (the Greek word *ekklesia* means gathering), citizens of his heaven and children of his kingdom. We are subject to his laws and directed by his Spirit. We do his bidding and establish his kingdom in his way and in his time.

> We form the very body of Christ so that he can carry on living his perfect life on earth through us

Just as the only valid ministry belongs to Jesus, so too the church belongs entirely to him. There is no such thing as 'my' church!

We have seen that Jesus' life was shot through with the Spirit. He was born of the Spirit, he lived in the Spirit, and he ministered in complete dependence on the Spirit. Then he baptized the church in the same Holy Spirit so that we can go on living with his purity, serving with his power and revealing the wonderful presence of God.

As we go on through this book, we will examine yet more closely the way that the Spirit works and how we can live and minister in the Spirit's presence today.

PART THREE

THE HOLY SPIRIT'S WORK TODAY

Right through from the first chapter of the Bible to the last, the Spirit is shown to be making a difference. Whether we see him as a hurricane wind or as another person like Jesus, we recognise that he is always bringing decisive change.

When we study the scriptures, it is easy to concentrate on only one or two of the changes which the Spirit makes. Sadly, some sections of the church focus almost exclusively on part of the Spirit's work – and miss out on some of the glories of his work.

For example, one group may emphasize his power for witness while another stresses his pure lifestyle, and a third group concentrates on the performance of spiritual gifts and specialist ministries.

If we want to be people who are saturated by the Spirit, who live only in his presence, it is important that we appreciate every facet of his work. We need to be hungry for *every* change that the Spirit wants to make in our individual and corporate lives. We should not try to dictate to him what he should do, or expect him to work in one particular area. We need to be ready for anything!

THE POWER OF THE SPIRIT

By now, we know that the Spirit is God's power in action. So, obviously, one main work of the Spirit is to bring power to those whom he fills.

In the Old Testament, when the Spirit fell on a select few, he caused them to break out in inspired speech. It is the same with the New Testament pre-Pentecost fillings. After their anointings, John, Elizabeth, Simeon, Zechariah, and Jesus all spoke with power and authority. People constantly remarked upon Jesus' powerful speech. Matthew 7:28-29, Mark 1:27, 6:1-3 & Luke 4:22, 32 illustrate this.

> They possessed experience, training and knowledge, but lacked the only acceptable qualification – power

We might think that disciples who had healed the sick, cast out demons, accompanied Jesus for three years and seen physical proof of his resurrection would be more than adequately equipped to be witnesses. This was not so.

They possessed experience, training and knowledge, but lacked the only acceptable qualification – power. In Luke 24:48-49 and Acts 1:4-8, Jesus promised that the anointing with the Spirit would remedy this deficiency. The book of

Acts is the result. Pentecost was the first fruit of the harvest. The three thousand completely converted in one day were the result of the power – with the promise of much more to follow.

The Greek word for power is usually *dunamis*: this describes a moral, physical or spiritual ability which resides in a person or object. It is the explosive energy which makes things happen!

Dunamis is the supernatural power of God by which miracles occur, preaching is made effective, and people are strengthened to endure terrible persecutions and adversity.

Please read this selection of New Testament passages and grasp the variety of ways that the Spirit brings *dunamis* power to Christian believers – and understand that these words are for us all today!. Acts 4:33; 6:8; 10:38; Romans 15:13-19; 1 Corinthians 2:4-5; 2 Corinthians 6:6-10, 10:4-6, 12:9; Ephesians 3:16, 6:10; Philippians 4:13; 1 Thessalonians 1:5; 2 Timothy 1:7, 3:4-5.

Power for proclamation

In the Old Testament, the Spirit gave prophets power to speak. They knew what to say and they had God's authority to say it. In the New Testament, the Spirit also enabled men and women to speak with a power and authority that they did not naturally possess.

Paul makes this clear in 1 Corinthians 2:4, 'My speech and my preaching were not with persuasive words of human wisdom, but in demonstration of the Spirit and of power'.

At Pentecost, the Spirit transformed the disciples'

> The Spirit enabled men and women to speak with a power and authority that they did not naturally possess

speaking. Acts 2:4 states, 'And they were all filled with the Holy Spirit and began to speak.... as the Spirit gave them utterance'. This prophetic speech – especially tongues – is still the key sign that somebody has been baptized in the Spirit.

> Believers have been changed from people whose words about Jesus are widely ignored, into those whose words have an enormous impact

Sometimes we focus too much on the supernatural gift of tongues at Pentecost. It matters far more that we realise the Spirit gave them the power prophetically to speak about 'the wonderful works of God' in a way which amazed and attracted their listeners. It was their powerful speech which proved that they had been filled with the Spirit.

This has been the testimony of God's people throughout history. By the anointing of the Spirit, believers have been changed from people whose words about Jesus are widely ignored, into those whose words have an enormous impact. They may say almost exactly the same things as before, but now with supernatural authority and power. This is what makes a vital difference to our evangelism. This sort of prophetic speech is the distinctive sign of the Spirit's anointing today.

Power for miracles

The prophets were the miracle workers of the Old Testament. Men like Moses, Elijah and Elisha – who had been filled with the Spirit – found not only that God empowered their speech, but that he also worked amazing miracles through them.

So it is in the New Testament. Because of the miracles, the people constantly assumed that Jesus was a prophet. They knew that the signs and wonders meant God was with Jesus in a special way. This is another key difference that the Spirit makes.

Acts 6:8 shows that power was the key to Stephen's miracles. And in Romans 15:18-19, Paul underlines that it is the power of God's Spirit: 'For I will not dare to speak of any of those things which Christ has not accomplished through me, in word and deed, to make the Gentiles obedient – in mighty signs and wonders, by the power of the Spirit of God, so that from Jerusalem and round about to Illyricum I have fully preached the gospel of Christ.'

It is important we grasp that the Spirit gives power for miracles essentially in the context of *evangelism*. Signs and wonders are mainly given to convince

> It is important we grasp that the Spirit gives power for miracles essentially in the context of evangelism

people that the message about Jesus is true. Of course God heals because he cares about sick and needy people, but he cares even more about their eternal destiny!

Some of the recent focus on miracles has focused too much on the healing of believers' minor ailments. As we will see, the power of the Spirit is given to help believers persevere in hardship, and to demonstrate to non-believers by miraculous signs that Jesus is alive. It is a fascinating study to read Acts and carefully note both the contexts and the consequences of the amazing miracles.

Power for warfare

We know that all Christians are involved in a titanic struggle with the forces of darkness. Sometimes we feel dreadfully weak and inadequate when we think about all the evil in the world, when we struggle with personal temptation, and when we try to answer people's objections to our faith.

Thank God that the Spirit gives us all the power we need for this spiritual warfare. 2 Corinthians 10:4-6 promises that 'the weapons of our warfare are not carnal but mighty in God for pulling down strongholds, casting down arguments and every high thing that exalts itself against the knowledge of God, bringing every thought into captivity to the obedience of Christ....'.

Time and again, we have to cry to God, begging him to help us, to strengthen us, to give us power to speak and act in the right way, to make us equal to the pressures we face.

Without exception, we all have to go on fighting evil in its many different forms – both within us and around us. It is crucial we understand that only the Spirit's power can give us victory. We will be defeated whenever we rely on our own resources or experience.

> **We will be defeated whenever we rely on our own resources or experience**

In Ephesians 3:16, Paul prays for his readers that God would grant them, 'according to the riches of his glory, to be strengthened with *dunamis* through his Spirit in the inner man'.

Surely this should still be a constant prayer both for ourselves and each other. We desperately need the Spirit's explosive power to help us push back the frontiers of evil in society and establish God's kingdom in our locality.

Power for victory

Some Christians see every difficulty as demonic activity, and seem to be obsessed with spiritual warfare. Yet many of the problems we face are just part and parcel of fallen humanity.

The devil is not necessarily the reason why rain falls on our washing, our car fails to start in the morning, we wake up with toothache, or next door's cat digs up our seedlings.

The ordinary problems of life can be overwhelming, but God does give us the grace and strength we need to overcome our weaknesses and troubles.

In 2 Corinthians 12:9-10, Paul records God's promise and his response. '"My grace is sufficient for you, for my strength is made perfect in weakness." Therefore I take pleasure in infirmities, in reproaches, in needs, in persecutions, in distresses, for Christ's sake. For when I am weak, then I am strong.'

Power for hope

Our observation and experience of society's breakdown, and our exposure to the media's constant reporting of the world's problems, can trigger real depression and despondency. We feel that everything is getting worse, and that there will never be an end to the hardships.

Most Christians know about God's glorious promises. But we need the power of the Spirit to translate these promises into a tangible experience which fills us with joyful hope in the face of yet more grim news.

> May the God of hope fill you with all joy and peace in believing, that you may abound in hope by the power of the Holy Spirit

We need to go on praying Paul's Romans 15:13 intercession for each other: 'May the God of hope fill you with all joy and peace in believing, that you may abound in hope by the power of the Holy Spirit.'

Power for perseverance

Western society increasingly demands instant solutions. The fashion is for 'fast' everything. If something breaks, it is discarded and replaced.

Many believers have been influenced by the world's pressure to seek quick solutions to their difficulties rather than God's power to persevere through hardships.

Please pause and read 2 Corinthians 6:3-10. This special passage helps us appreciate Paul's attitude to difficult circumstances. He knew the truth that God gives patience and grace to endure troubles. Remember, the gift of God's strength for endurance is often God's way for us to overcome our personal and family hardships.

> God's strength for endurance is often his way for us to overcome hardships

Colossians 1:11 promises that we are 'strengthened with all might, according to his glorious power, for all patience, long-suffering with joy'.

It is the power of the humble Spirit which stiffens our resolve to persevere. It is the *Paraclete* – 'the Encourager' – who urges us to keep going in adversity. It is 'the Spirit of Truth' who teaches us to recognise that patience produces faith, and to reject worldly thinking and attitudes.

Power for the church

Ephesians 1:19-23 is one of the greatest New Testament descriptions of God's power – and makes it clear that God gives power essentially within the context of the church.

In recent years, there has been a tremendous emphasis in western society on the individual. Unfortunately this has spread into the church, and many leaders have over-stressed the importance of our individual response to God.

This truth must be complemented by the New Testament focus on our corporate response, relationships and activities.

Generally, the word 'you' in the New Testament means a plural 'you all' rather than a singular 'you on your own'.

The promises of God are more for us together than they are for us apart. This is why the pictures of the church describe one united entity – the body, the bride, the temple, and so on – rather than many small separated units.

Ephesians 1:19-23 is a healthy reminder that God's power is given mainly in a church setting. It is the church against which the gates of hell cannot prevail – not isolated individual believers.

This means that our prayers for power should be 'give us' rather than 'give me'!

Power for witness

If we tried to wrap together all the different reasons why the Spirit gives us his power, we would surely have to come to a verse like Acts 4:33. 'And with great power the apostles gave witness to the resurrection of the Lord Jesus. And great grace was upon them all.'

> The test of true spiritual power is whether it brings people into a deep knowledge and understanding of Jesus

The Spirit gives us power to proclaim and to persevere, for miracles and warfare, in order that we will become powerful witnesses to the risen Lord Jesus.

Miracles are not only to bless us. Victory and hope are not only to make our lives more comfortable. They are to provide an eloquent and effective testimony for others.

Power to know Jesus better

Every aspect of the Spirit's power is given to enable us to know Jesus better, and to help us reveal Jesus more clearly to the world around us. The real test of true spiritual power is whether or not it brings people into a deep knowledge and understanding of Jesus.

Jesus' stark warning in Matthew 7:15-23 shows clearly that the ability to cast out demons, to prophesy, to perform miracles is not enough on its own.

When spiritual power does not bring people close to Jesus; when the motive behind a ministry is selfish, or obedience and truth are absent, or the focus is on a 'Man of God'; whenever there is mere 'performance' – it is the Simon spirit we read about in Acts 8:9-24.

In that chapter we see the temptation for power divorced from truth, holiness and moral purity. We see the desire for power both as an end in itself and as a means to an end.

The story of Acts 8 has been repeated endlessly down through the centuries – and is still one of the devil's main tricks today.

> Too many believers pray for power for reasons *other* than knowing Jesus better and revealing him more clearly

Too many believers are praying for power for reasons *other* than knowing Jesus better and revealing him more clearly. And too many leaders are trying to manipulate divine power at their own will, when they should be experiencing the Spirit's power as they obey God's will.

The Spirit does bring breathtaking changes through his *dunamis* power. He does provide us with the strength and ability to do what we know we ought to do. This empowering from Christ through the Spirit is a glorious truth which we should want to experience more and more.

But only so that we may know Jesus better. And only that we may reveal him more clearly. We must grasp that the Spirit's power is given to turn us into better witnesses, into men and women whose words and lives – whose every-day behaviour and spiritual authority – show that Jesus Christ really is alive.

THE PURITY OF THE SPIRIT

Although we often talk about 'the Spirit', we know that he is rightly called 'the *Holy* Spirit'. His name reveals his nature – he is perfect holiness.

The second great work of the Spirit is bringing purity and holiness into our lives. Through the Spirit, God cleanses us from sin's pollution by helping us to resist temptation and to do what is right.

Romans 8:13-14 introduces the first stage in this work of the Spirit: 'If you live according to the flesh you will die; but if by the Spirit you put to death the deeds of the body, you will live. For as many as are led by the Spirit of God, these are the sons of God'.

> Through the Spirit, God cleanses us from sin's pollution by helping us to resist temptation, and do what is right

2 Corinthians 3:18 describes the second stage. 'But we all, with unveiled face, beholding as in a mirror the glory of the Lord, are being transformed into the same image from glory to glory, just as by the Spirit of the Lord.'

Purity from sin

Nearly every aspect of the Spirit's work is 'foreshadowed' or introduced in the Old Testament. We have seen that the Spirit enabled the prophets to speak God's words with power and authority, and therefore can expect to find passages which show him purging God's people from sin.

Isaiah 61:8 is set in a great chapter about the Spirit's work, and it shows that God hates sin. Isaiah 4:4 looks forward to a time when Israel will have been washed and purged 'by the spirit of judgment and by the spirit of burning'. Zechariah 13:1 prophecies that a day will come when sin and uncleanness will be dealt with by 'a fountain'.

God in his grace is determined to forgive our sinful behaviour – and to end it

Ezekiel 36:25-27 contains this important Old Testament promise of God. 'I will sprinkle clean water on you, and you shall be clean; I will cleanse you from all your filthiness and from your idols. I will give you a new heart and put a new spirit within you; I will take the heart of stone out of your flesh and give you a heart of flesh. I will put my Spirit within you and cause you to walk in my statutes, and you will keep my judgments and do them.'

These verses help us to appreciate that sinful behaviour makes us dirty before God. It repels him – in the same way that we are repelled by filth which ought not to be present. However, the verses show that God in his grace is also determined to forgive our sinful behaviour – and to end it.

All the Old Testament purity laws and rituals point to God's cleansing work. This is seen even more clearly in the New Testament descriptions of salvation, especially in those which describe washing and cleansing (John 13:10; 15:3; Acts 22:16; 1 Corinthians 6:11; 2 Corinthians 7:1; Ephesians 5:3-5, 25-27; 2 Timothy 2:20-22; Hebrews 9:11-14; 10:22; 1 John 1:7-9; 3:3).

The Spirit is God's agent of purity. He makes us 'born again'. He provides us with the new heart which enables us to live in purity and to obey God's commandments. He shapes our lives and regenerates us. He enables us to receive the very nature of Christ – and to become more and more like him throughout our earthly lives.

Of course we know that none of this is automatic – outside our free-will. When we receive the Spirit we neither become all-powerful nor instantly all-perfect. Our pilgrimage to power and purity is a life-long struggle which means on-going tension and incomplete achievement: 'For the flesh lusts against the Spirit, and the Spirit against the flesh; and these are contrary to one another, so that you do not do the things that you wish' (Galatians 5:17).

However the Spirit is very active in a wide variety of ways, slowly working purity into the lives of believers.

Purity through strength to change

The Spirit of truth makes as aware of our faults and failings. He draws our attention to the different ways we disappoint God. He highlights our bad habits. And he gives us all the inner strength we need to 'cleanse ourselves from all filthiness of the flesh and spirit, perfecting holiness in the fear of God' (2 Corinthians 7:1).

Two of the devil's favourite tactics are tempting us to try and do what God alone can do, and tricking us into asking God to do what he has told us to do!

It is important we understand that there are two strands to the New Testament purity teaching. There is one element of cleansing which God does through the Spirit, and there is another element which he expects us to carry out ourselves – again, through the Spirit.

> One part of cleansing is done by God through the Spirit. But there is a second element which we must carry out ourselves through the Spirit

Romans 8:13-14 makes it clear that 'by the Spirit' we are called to 'put to death the deeds of the body'. God won't do this for us; he won't even do it through us; instead, he enables us to do it ourselves – by the Spirit!

This means that we should always be moving forward in the Spirit, developing godly habits in every area of our lives. Every year we should become a little more like Christ as we 'serve in the newness of the Spirit' (Romans 7:6).

Romans 6:17-7:6, Galatians 5:13 & 1 Thessalonians 4:1-8 show that holiness is God's will for all our lives. Because we have received the Spirit, we can 'put to death the deeds of the body', and we can 'walk according the Spirit'.

Every day, we all feel both the Holy Spirit's desires and our own fleshly desires. The devil makes us think that we are the only believers who are facing this struggle, that some Christians just don't have any fleshly desires. It's not true. We all have to struggle hard to follow the Spirit's leading and ignore our own desires.

Some people think that it will get easier as they grow older and more mature in the faith. But as we follow the Spirit we keep on discovering that we are not as good as we should be. We find that we have to go on depending on God's grace and mercy, that sin and selfish ambition keep on tainting much

> **We all have to struggle to follow the Spirit's leading and ignore our own desires**

of what we do; and that – right to the end of our lives – we are always needing to cry out to the Spirit to strengthen our resolve to stay on the path of holiness.

Purity through transformation

The good news is that our spiritual struggle is not self-effort. As we have seen, another strand of purity teaching runs through the New Testament. Many verses testify that we *are* washed, cleansed and sanctified. God, by the Spirit, works in our lives to bring purity, to shape us in his image.

2 Corinthians 3:18 states that 'we all are being trans-

formed into the same image .... by the Spirit'. The image is that of Christ himself. As we walk in the Spirit, we are changed by the Spirit so that progressively we reflect the Lord's glory and are transformed into his image.

Few passages describe this transformation more beautifully than Galatians 5:22-24. Here, Paul paints a word-picture of the truly Christ-like character which comes to those who are living in the Spirit.

> As we walk in the Spirit, we are changed by the Spirit so that progressively we reflect the Lord's glory and are transformed into his image

'The fruit of the Spirit is love, joy, peace, long-suffering, kindness, goodness, faithfulness, gentleness, self-control. Against such there is no law. And those who are Christ's have crucified the flesh with its passions and desires.'

This is not a list of a great variety of fruits, rather it is the fullest possible description of one particular fruit – the one nature of Christ. Just as ordinary fruit naturally develops on healthy, mature trees which are living in the right conditions, so this spiritual fruit naturally develops in believers who are living in the right place – in the Spirit.

This is no instant transformation. It is a slow but persistent change which God brings to the lives of those who 'have crucified the flesh with its passions and desires'.

In this important passage, Paul ties together the two strands of purity teaching. Our responsibility, by the Spirit, is to resist our selfish fleshly desires. God's gift to us, in the Spirit, is a complete change of nature.

The two strands must stand together. People who focus too much on 'crucifying the flesh' tend to become legalistic – more concerned with detailed principles than the love of Christ. Whereas those who sit around waiting for the fruit to grow tend to be casual about sin and holiness – they fail fully to appreciate God's repulsion from every form of sin.

Purity for witness

Time and again we have seen that the Spirit's main work is bringing glory to Jesus, focusing the world's attention on him, drawing sinful people into the love and grace of God.

In the same way that the main purpose of his power is to convince people of the truth about Jesus, the main reason of his purity is to show people the nature of Jesus.

> We are given the gift of purity so that the people around us will see and be drawn to Jesus

We are called to be pure and are given the gift of purity so that people around us will see and be drawn to Jesus. Too often, however, there is a gap between what we Christians say and what we do: the world considers this to be hypocrisy.

Few things cause people to turn more quickly from God than sinful believers – especially those who seem to claim to be far better than they really are.

And little draws people closer to Jesus than ordinary lives which radiate God's love and reveal Christ's character.

Purity, like power, is for witness. Practical holiness must exist in our lives if our evangelism is to be effective! But it needs to stand alongside the full power of the Spirit. The Spirit wants to change us from fallen, fallible men and women into powerful, pure sons and daughters of God.

Power and Purity

We cannot choose between power and purity. It is both or neither, not one or the other! Of course, some Christians do seem to focus solely on either power or purity, but there is great danger in doing this. An over-concentration on power leads to a Simon the Sorceror spirit, whereas too close a focus on purity leads to the joyless legalism of the Pharisees.

In Matthew 23:23 and Luke 18:9-14, Jesus condemned the Pharisees because their hearts were not right with God. The Pharisees had started out as a group of people who were offended by the paganism and immorality of their culture. They had wanted to return to godly standards of purity and morality. But what began in holiness degenerated into legalism and hypocrisy.

They had focused on purity and forgotten the power of God. They concentrated on rules, and did not know the heart of God. They became judgmental and self-righteous.

We must guard against this today. Not only does it displease God, it also – as 2 Timothy 3:5 shows – turns people away. The Holy Spirit is bringing a new wave of holiness into the church,

> What began in holiness degenerated into legalism and hypocrisy

and Satan will try to corrupt it with this sort of moralism and legalism.

Somehow we need to maintain a balance between power and purity in our lives and congregations – and the easiest way to do this is by embracing them both as fully as possible!

However, there is a third work of the Spirit which – when grasped – greatly helps us stay close to God's heart and be effective witnesses to the needy people who live around us.

THE PRESENCE OF THE SPIRIT

We have looked at how the Holy Spirit brings power and purity into our lives. Both are important. Both have their dangers. And neither on their own is the definitive work of the Holy Spirit in today's church.

The third great change that the Spirit makes is undoubtedly the most important one of all. It is wonderful that the Spirit releases the power of God into our lives. It is glorious that the Spirit transforms us with the purity of God. But far more wonderful is the fact that he brings the very presence of God into our personal and corporate lives.

It is the work of the Holy Spirit to bring or mediate the presence of Christ to the church – in power and purity. It is his special work to make known the personal presence of the risen Lord Jesus – the Jesus of history, the Jesus of heaven – in and with the church and individual believers.

> **It is his work to make known the personal presence of the risen Lord Jesus in and with the church and individual believers**

When we walk with the Spirit, when we experience the presence of Christ that he brings, we will have his resurrection power and his holy purity.

Ever since the day of Pentecost, the Spirit has been present with believers, changing them to reveal God more clearly so that Christ may be better known and praised.

Like most aspects of the Spirit's work, this is foreshadowed in the Old Testament. Many passages – like Psalm 139 – describe God's universal presence. But there are several examples of God being present with a person to bless them in a special way.

Genesis 39:2; Exodus 3:12; 33:14-16; Deuteronomy 31:6-8; Joshua 1:5,9; & Isaiah 43:2 describe God being *with* his people in a way which enables them to be bold and strong.

Naturally, this is fulfilled in Jesus – who is introduced by

Matthew 1:23 as the ultimate 'God with us', the Emmanuel of Isaiah 7.

It promised a degree of intimacy with the Godhead which had only been experienced before in Eden

Having described Jesus throughout in terms of power and righteousness, Matthew ends his gospel by returning to the idea of Jesus as Emmanuel: 'and lo, I am with you always, even to the end of the age' (28:20).

Jesus is God with us. His presence is the presence of God. Yet Jesus disappeared soon after he made his Matthew 28:20 promise. He has not been present on earth in the flesh since his ascension. However, his promise was fulfilled by the coming of the Holy Spirit – the *Paraclete*, the another just like Jesus.

Physically, Jesus is at the right hand of the Father in heaven until the day when he comes again. But, spiritually, he is now present on earth in the person of the Holy Spirit.

John 14:23 is one of the most wonderful biblical promises: 'If anyone loves me, he will keep my word; and my Father will love him, and we will come to him and make our home with him'. Jesus promised a degree of intimacy with the Godhead which had only been experienced before in Eden.

Yet this promise came directly after Jesus had promised not to leave his followers orphans but to give them *another Paraclete* – the Helper who is exactly the same as him.

Jesus is teaching about the Holy Spirit in John 14:23. Jesus is saying that the Spirit will bring the very presence of *both* the Father and the Son. In the Spirit, the full Godhead will make its home, its permanent earthly residence, in Jesus' human disciples.

The presence of Jesus

Paul makes it plain in 2 Corinthians 3:17-18 that Jesus comes to us through the Holy Spirit. 'Now the Lord is the Spirit; and where the Spirit of the Lord is, there is liberty. But we all, with unveiled face, beholding as in a mirror the glory of the Lord, are being transformed into the same image from glory to glory, just as by the Spirit of the Lord.'

Paul is not confusing the Holy Spirit with Jesus, rather he is explaining that we know the presence of Jesus through a vital living relationship with the Spirit.

It is precisely the same in passages like Romans 8:9; Galatians 4:6; Philippians 1:19 and 1 Peter 1:11. Please read them and see how the indwelling of the Spirit is equated with belonging to Christ.

Everything Jesus says to us or does through us is accomplished by the Spirit – because Jesus is present by the Spirit. The presence of the Spirit is the presence of Christ – and vice versa. This means that we will commit ourselves to developing and maintaining a relationship with the Spirit if we are serious about knowing Jesus better.

> Everything Jesus says to us or does through us is accomplished by the Spirit – because Jesus is present by the Spirit

The most basic ministry of the Spirit is to mediate Christ's presence to us. He provides us with the knowledge of Jesus' presence in many different ways, but we should find that three things keep on happening as we enjoy the presence of Jesus through the Spirit.

The fellowship of his presence

In John 16:12-14, Jesus explains how the Holy Spirit takes the things of Jesus and makes them known to us. 'I still have many things to say to you, but you cannot bear them now. However, when he, the Spirit of truth, has come, he will guide you into all truth; for he will not speak on his own authority, but whatever he hears he will speak, and he will tell you things to come.'

Jesus' first followers walked and talked with Jesus. They listened to his voice, learnt from his words and actions, felt his love, and lived in close fellowship with him.

> As we listen to the Spirit, we hear the words and voice of Jesus – reminding us of his love and guiding our thoughts and actions

This intimate fellowship with Jesus still continues today as we experience his presence through the Holy Spirit. When we listen to the Spirit, we hear the words and voice of Jesus – reminding us of his love and guiding our thoughts and actions. We can see this in Revelation 2 & 3, where Jesus' personal message is 'what the Spirit says to the churches'.

Of course, most believers don't hear Jesus audibly. But the Spirit speaks to us through God's word, other believers, God's creation, spiritual gifts and our own inner spirit.

The transformation of his presence

We all recognise that men and women are influenced by the people with whom they spend a great deal of time. It is the same with Jesus. The more time we spend in his presence, in the Spirit, the more we become like him. The longer we listen to his words, the more they control our thoughts – and so on. We can see this in 2 Corinthians 3:18.

When we saturate ourselves in the four gospels, gazing at Jesus to grasp his attitudes and motives, we can begin to appreciate how we should think and behave. But we will not begin to be transformed until we are actually in the presence of Jesus – until Jesus is in us by the Spirit – moulding our motives and energising our will.

We have seen that Jesus' ministry had several main themes. He called people to obey him as king, to depend on him as saviour, to follow his perfect pattern life, and to worship him as holy God. In the Spirit, Jesus is present both in and with us in all these aspects.

The king of kings, the conqueror of evil, the ruler over sickness, the judge of the whole earth – he is with us. We live in his presence. Nothing we think or do is missed by him. By the Spirit, the king speaks to us. His presence is bound to transform us!

> We will not begin to be transformed until Jesus is in us by the Spirit, moulding our motives and energising our will

The suffering servant of humanity, the gentle shepherd who lay down his life for his sheep, the blood-stained substitute who bore God's wrath against sin – he too is with us. We live in his presence. By the Spirit, the suffering servant points out his sacrificial way of living and dying. Surely his presence will make a difference.

The ideal human being, the perfect specimen of humanity, the pattern life for all mankind, the sympathising friend of sinners – he is with us. In the Spirit, we live with him and he lives with us. By the Spirit, the Son of Man shows us that he really does understand our weaknesses – but still accepts us and urges us to go on following him more nearly.

The glorious light-bearing, life-bringing Son of God, the living Word, the complete revelation of the invisible Father – he is with us in the Spirit. Even as we read this, we are living in his holy presence. By the Spirit, the living God fellowships with us. It is almost too much to bear – and it just must make a difference to our lives. How can we be in the presence of Jesus in this way and remain unchanged?

The assurance of his presence

In Romans 8:16, Paul promises that 'the Spirit himself bears witness with our Spirit that we are children of God, and if children, then heirs – heirs of God and joint heirs with Christ'.

The presence of Jesus in and with us by the Spirit is proof that we are loved and accepted by God. The presence of the Spirit is the 'seal' which assures us that we have been forgiven, redeemed, reconciled and welcomed into God's family.

> The presence of the Spirit is the seal which assures us that we have been forgiven, redeemed, reconciled and welcomed into God's family

In Genesis 8:9-14, the dove brought Noah assurance that God had not forgotten him. It was full of promise. The descent of the Spirit at Jesus' baptism was related to the voice which gave Jesus assurance of his Sonship, the Father's love and divine pleasure.

Hebrews 10:15-16 also makes clear the Spirit's work of assurance. Our doubts start to fade when the Spirit reveals the very presence of God to us. We know because we know. A deep, unbreakable certainty of adoption, an immovable conviction of the Father's love is experienced which makes circumstances seem irrelevant. This is not obstinate arrogance, it is the work of the Spirit.

The presence of God

Many people around us have some sort of belief in a God who is 'out there somewhere'. What they see in creation and what they feel inside themselves convinces them that some sort of supernatural being must exist. They don't know him. They have some very strange ideas about him. But deep down – even if only when faced with a crisis – most people believe in a God who is there.

People of all religions believe in a God who is tangibly real, and credit him with varying degrees of power and benevolence. Christianity is different. For on top of our belief in the living God who is everywhere, who made and sustains all things, we uniquely claim that he is here with us.

> The coming of the Spirit means that we enjoy not only the presence of Jesus, but also the presence of the Father

We know that Jesus was the perfect revelation of the invisible God, and therefore understand that knowing Jesus means we must also know the Father.

Jesus came to reconcile us with the Father, to 'bridge the gap' between us and God. This means the Spirit reveals not just the Son to us, but – through the Son – the Father.

Jesus makes this particularly clear in John 14:23: 'we will come to him and make *our* home in him'. The coming of the Spirit means that we enjoy not only the presence of Jesus, but also the presence of the Father.

This is what Paul describes in 2 Corinthians 4:6 when he writes about Jesus as the light which shines 'in our hearts to give the light of the knowledge of the glory of God in the face of Jesus Christ'.

Since Pentecost, the Spirit has been actively revealing the presence of God. Although it may be easy – even fashionable – for Christians to talk about power and purity, we need to understand that there can be no greater change, no more important change, than revealing the presence of God in our dark and evil world.

Although the New Testament makes much of the Spirit's power and purity, it makes even more of him mediating the presence, the word and the activity of God. Please read this selection of passages to gain an overview of this aspect of the Spirit's work: Luke 3:22, 4:1, 14, 18, 10:21; John 1:32-33; 3:34; 14:16; 18-21; 15:26; 16:7; 20:22; Acts 2:33; 10:38; 16:7; Romans 8:9-11; Galatians 4:6; Philippians 1:19; 1 Peter 1:11; 1 John 2:20, 27.

The presence for glory

In the Old Testament, the expression 'the glory of God' is used in two ways. It refers to the self-revealed character of God, and to a visible revelation of God's presence. This means that God's glory shows people where God is and what he is like: it is the outward manifestation of his absolute holiness.

God's glory appeared to the seventy elders on Mount Sinai (Exodus 24); his glory was regularly seen in the wilderness tabernacle at the hour of sacrifice (Leviticus 9:6-24); and it filled the Jerusalem Temple (1 Kings 8:1-11).

In the New Testament, these aspects of God's glory were perfectly fulfilled in Christ: he is both

> God's glory shows people where God is and what he is like

the complete self-revelation of God's character and also the clearest revelation of God's presence.

The word 'glory' normally describes Jesus' revelation of God's nature by grace and miracles. It adds to the Old Testament the sense of a demonstration of beautiful perfection and a display of magnificent power. God's glory seen in Jesus shows the Father's splendid excellence and the full extent of his authority and power.

Since Pentecost, it has been the church's function to

> **When we pray for God's glory to be seen, we are asking for the world to see his holiness, grace and power**

reveal God's great glory in and to the world. This means that we are meant to be showing God's holy character to the world, to be being seen by the world as the place where God resides, and to be demonstrating God's regal authority and power.

By now we should realise that we can only glorify God by being full of the presence of God – and that is the greatest work of the Spirit.

When we pray for God's glory to be seen, we are asking for the world to see his holiness, grace and power – and they see that in us through the Spirit's work. As he brings God's presence to us, so God is glorified in the world through us.

His presence for witness

Jesus' words about the Holy Spirit in John 14-16 introduce the Spirit's work of bringing glory to Jesus. However 'glory' has become such a 'religious' word – one that is used mostly in worship – that we sometimes forget this word is mainly about witness.

Please reread John 14-16, looking out for the different strands of the Spirit's work we've examined. Power, purity, presence, glory are there. But pay special attention to the evangelistic heart which beats through these chapters.

In John 15:26, Jesus states that the *Paraclete* will be his witness – and that we will also be his witnesses. It is impossible to separate the work of the Spirit from witness. Everything he does is a witness to Jesus. Every change that he brings to our lives is meant to make us better witnesses to Jesus.

He gives us power so people will believe that Jesus has risen from the dead. He makes us holy so that our behaviour does not cause folk to stumble. And he brings the presence of Jesus to our lives so that, wherever we are, we reveal God's glorious nature.

The Spirit takes the things of Christ and makes them know to us: this brings glory to Jesus. He does this through a vital, living, personal relationship which he continually seeks to establish with us.

Christ will be glorified in us when we develop and maintain this relationship with the Spirit. We will know Jesus, we will know the Father, we will walk in the

> Every change that he brings to our lives is meant to make us better witnesses to Jesus

ways of God, and – most important of all – we will be accurate and effective witnesses in the world to the living Lord Jesus.

PERFORMANCE AND THE SPIRIT

We have looked at the three main works of the Spirit: power, purity, and – most importantly – the presence of God.

However, some believers appear to suggest that spiritual performance is central to the Spirit's work today. Their focus is on the use of spiritual gifts in meetings and services, on participation by as many people as possible, on special worship and Christian activities.

All of these things are good and right, and they often are a consequence of the Spirit's work. But they are not at the heart of the Spirit. He is concerned with revealing Jesus more brightly through the life of every individual believer and through the corporate life of the church. Spiritual gifts and special activities are part of this, but not to the exclusion of presence, power and purity.

The performance of spiritual gifts

We have seen that spiritual gifts are very important. We know that they are tools to get a particular job done – supernatural abilities which the Spirit makes available to all believers who are living in him so that the kingdom of God can be promoted.

But remember, they are *gifts*, not rewards. They do not prove anything except God's essential graciousness and the Spirit's reality.

There are well-known gifts in Romans 12:6-8; 1 Corinthians 12:7-10 & Ephesians 4:8-11; lesser known gifts in 1 Corinthians 7:7; 13:3 & 1 Peter 4:9-10; and other less-obvious gifts – like leading worship – which are not mentioned in the New Testament.

> **They are supernatural abilities which the Spirit makes available to all believers who are living in him so that the kingdom of God can be promoted**

These gifts may be supernatural enhancements of our natural abilities or something entirely new. Either way, through them, the Spirit equips us to do something beautiful and purposeful for God.

He chooses which gifts to give to each believer. Romans 12:3; Hebrews 2:4 and 1 Corinthians 12:11 show God's sovereignty. And 1 Corinthians 12:31; 14:1 & 14:12 show that we need to cultivate a desire to be used by God, and a readiness and willingness to build up other people.

In the past thirty years, thousands of books have been written about the gifts, countless conferences have been held, innumerable sermons preached – all explaining how the gifts can be received, recognised, used and developed.

This has mainly been the Spirit of truth drawing us back to supernatural Christianity. Inevitably, however, the devil has tried to distort, confuse, corrupt and spoil God's work.

Spiritual gifts are not the sum total of the Spirit's work. Performance is not the essence of life in the Spirit. Vast numbers of gifts in a person or

> We need to cultivate a desire to be used by God, and a readiness and willingness to build up other people

congregation do not mean spiritual maturity or fruitfulness. Matthew 7:21-23 shows that they neither prove we are pleasing God nor guarantee our salvation.

Paul's first letter to the church in Corinth commends their gifts but rebukes their immaturity, sinfulness and lack of love. It is a terrible distortion of the Spirit's objective for the church when there are gifts without graces, charisma without character, performance without presence.

Of course the Spirit wants us to make very good use of his gifts – that's why he gives them. But he wants us to use them in his way, at his prompting – the focus is on obedience rather than performance, on living in the Spirit rather than performing for the Spirit.

The performance of body ministries

For centuries, the church had assumed that very few Christians were equipped for ministry. Full-time male clergy and a tiny number of others were thought to be the only people whom God wanted to use in helping, teaching and reaching other people.

In recent years, the Spirit of truth has restored the truth to the church that every member in the body of Christ has a vital ministry role.

We have seen that this is an important biblical truth. Vast numbers of Christians have been released into ministry. Apostles, prophets, evangelists, pastors and teachers have begun to appreciate that they are meant to equip God's people for the work of service. A greater freedom, flexibility and readiness to experiment has developed.

But, naturally, the devil has tried to ruin this lovely work of the Spirit. Some Christians have over-emphasized this truth and made the performance of ministry the focus of their teaching about the Spirit.

Of course God has a role for everyone. Of course God wants us all to take part in ministry. Of course the Spirit wants us to pass on God's words and love to others. But the heart of his ministry is revealing Jesus, making him better known, bringing glory to God, filling our lives with purity and power.

> He wants us to grasp his heart, to share his objective, not to be side-tracked by an interest in structures and small details

Spiritual gifts and body ministry are means to a greater end, they are not objectives to be attained. They are consequences of the Spirit's work, not the main thrust. He most certainly wants to use these things to reveal Jesus. But he wants us to grasp his heart, to share his objective, not to be side-tracked by an interest in structures and small details.

The performance of Christian activities

In the last twenty years there has been a fantastic multiplying of Christian activities. Churches have been inspired by the Holy Spirit to reach into their communities in a host of caring ways.

Vast numbers of works have been begun among the elderly and young mothers. Schemes have been launched to help the unemployed, the disabled, the housebound and the homeless. New societies have started. Groups of talented believers have pioneered artistic companies. And many congregations have spent much more time on their services – prayerfully developing their worship into more creative and contemporary patterns.

> God is more concerned with the internal than the external, with ethics than activity, with motives than deeds

Most of these ventures have been prompted by the Spirit. Nearly all have begun with the right and holy aim of revealing Christ's love and power to a broken world.

Yet Satan is trying to corrupt and distract the people who are involved in all these things. He tempts us to make them an end in themselves, so that – for example – we are more concerned with performing the activity than with pleasing God.

The problem with any stress on performance – whether gifts, ministries or activities – is that God is always more concerned with the internal than the external, with ethics than activity, with motives than deeds.

What matters is being like Jesus. Passages like Philippians 2:1-11 and Romans 12:1-3 remind us that submission to God and sensitivity to each other are vitally important.

Read Paul's prayers and see how he intercedes that we will be filled with knowledge, strength and blameless purity – not that we will be enabled by the Spirit to perform amazing exploits: 2 Corinthians 13:9; Ephesians1:17-18, 3:14-19; Philippians 1:9-11; Colossians 1:9-11; 1 Thessalonians 3:12-13; 2 Thessalonians1:11-12; Philemon 6.

It is a terrible temptation to measure the Spirit's work in us by the number of activities we are involved with, and by our skill and success in performing them.

All our Spirit-inspired activities should be humble acts of serving God – that is their only importance. We must never think or suggest that actions which are dramatic or eye-catching, which are public and impressive, are more important than lesser or more private actions.

> **Submission to God and sensitivity to each other are what really matter**

We are doomed to spiritual disappointment unless we fully grasp that the main changes the Spirit wants to make are to fill us with the presence of God, to help us know Jesus better and make him better known, and to transform us with purity and power into more accurate witnesses.

THE PROGRAMME OF THE SPIRIT

Too many believers today think about the Holy Spirit in a way which is far removed from the New Testament. They view him as a means of solving their problems, and come to him hoping for a thrilling personal experience.

Some readers of this book may even be thinking that the Holy Spirit is primarily concerned to make *them* pure and powerful.

As we think about the exciting work of the Spirit across the world, it is easy to express his activity in human-centered words. We start talking about what he is doing to us and to our church, what he wants leaders to say and do – and so on. Yet this misses the main thrust of the Spirit's ministry today – for there is only one item on his agenda.

To glorify Jesus

At the last supper, Jesus introduced the *Paraclete* in words which must be central to our understanding of the Spirit:

'He will testify of me' (John 15:26), and 'He will glorify me' (John 16:14).

At Pentecost, when Jesus baptized the church in the Holy Spirit and empowered the first believers for service, the crowds were interested in the tongues, the wind and the fire. However, Peter did not preach a message which offered them this experience, instead he said 'Hear these words: Jesus of Nazareth, a man attested by God to you....'.

The simplest possible definition of the Spirit's work today is 'He glorifies Jesus'. Every activity of the Spirit, every effect of the Spirit, every ministry and gift of the Spirit needs to be understood and interpreted within that basic definition.

We will miss God's heart if we fail to appreciate the primary purpose of all the Spirit's actions today. We won't grasp what the Spirit is doing if we don't understand why he is doing it.

There is only one answer to the question 'What is the Spirit doing today?' He is glorifying Jesus. Whatever else he is doing – whether shaking the church, restoring a neglected truth, purifying sinful leaders, and so on – he is doing it as a means to the end of bringing glory to Jesus.

> We won't grasp what the Spirit is doing if we don't understand why he is doing it

Some people will want to ask why the Spirit does this. There are two answers.

Firstly, Jesus is glorious. He thoroughly deserves all the worship, love, praise, adoration, attention and loyalty that the Spirit gives him. When we draw close to Jesus, we will naturally want to join the Spirit in giving all our love and devotion to Jesus. In eternally glorifying Jesus, the Holy

There is only one answer to the question 'What is the Spirit doing today?' He is glorifying Jesus

Spirit is only doing the most natural and self-evident thing in the universe.

Secondly, it is the Father's good purpose. He wants the Son to be known, to be loved, to be obeyed, to be relied upon, to be followed, to be served, to have first place in everything. In humbly doing all to bring glory to Jesus, the Spirit is simply obeying the Father's will for his life.

To bring the presence of Jesus

If there is only one item on the Spirit's agenda, he also has only one main way of carrying it out. If he exists to bring glory to Jesus, to testify to Jesus, he accomplishes this by bringing – by mediating – Christ's presence.

Although Jesus is in heaven, he is here by the Spirit. The Spirit glorifies Jesus by revealing him, by presenting him, by speaking his words and performing his deeds.

Through the Spirit, Jesus approaches and addresses us. He loves and encourages us, he guides and directs us. But, of course, Jesus' presence by the Spirit is not passive. Through the Spirit he is dynamically active.

He urges us into powerful action – pressing us to deal with demons, evil and sickness; to heal the broken-hearted, feed the hungry, clothe the naked, visit the imprisoned; to go about doing those deeds that he directs.

He transforms us into a more pure way of living and thinking – making us aware of our shortcomings, strengthening our resolve, sharpening our minds, supporting us under pressure, shaping us in his own glorious image.

The Spirit's work is to glorify Jesus, and he does this essentially by bringing the presence of Jesus to us. He will do *anything* to create, develop, sustain and heighten our awareness of Jesus.

He regenerates us. He sanctifies us. He speaks to us through the Scriptures, through leaders, in the quiet of our own minds. He assures us of our eternal destiny. He gives us supernatural gifts and abilities. He pours God's power into our lives. He challenges our lethargy. He helps us in our weaknesses. He gives us faith. He helps us to pray. He fills us with perseverance and hope. He rebukes and corrects us. He challenges our thinking.

> He will do *anything* to create, develop, sustain and heighten our awareness of Jesus

He does all this in order that we may know Jesus better and may make him better known. And he does this so that the living Lord Jesus is glorified in the world around us today.

Submitting to the Spirit

Yet just as we've seen that the spiritual life is not self-effort, so it is not passivity. We are not called to do nothing while we wait for the Spirit to glorify Jesus through us. Rather, we need to respond to his work by actively submitting to his will and prompting.

Jesus submits to the Father, and the Spirit submits to Jesus. They do this in the context of a wonderful living, loving, trusting relationship.

Our response to the Spirit's work – to his desire to glorify Jesus in us and through us – should be to pursue a dynamic and beautiful relationship with him which is based on our complete dependence, our total submission, to his holy will and work.

When we do this, we really will be starting to live in the presence of the living God. The final section of this book should help you begin to develop just such a special and intimate relationship with the Holy Spirit – which, in turn, will enable you to reach out with God's love to some of the needy people around you.

PART FOUR

LIVING WITH THE HOLY SPIRIT

At the end of many meetings and services, Christian people frequently bless each other with Paul's famous 2 Corinthians 13:14 prayer. 'The grace of the Lord Jesus Christ, and the love of God, and the fellowship of the Holy Spirit be with you all.'

When the Bible speaks about Jesus, the main word is grace. When it describes God, its central idea is love. And when it introduces the Spirit, its key word is *fellowship*.

The Greek word for this is *koinonia*. Some versions of the Bible translate this as communion, but it literally means 'sharing in something together'.

The idea of 'fellowship' has been horribly devalued by

its use in Christian groups. For many believers, it means little more than a chat over coffee after a service. Yet *koinonia* means sharing closely together in something active.

It is the word for a partnership which has a clear common purpose. Fellowship is active not passive. It's dynamic, not insipid. It involves communication, co-operation, contribution, direction, action and accomplishment. Genuine scriptural *koinonia* partnership/fellowship always has a goal, and always has an outcome.

It is not enough to say that we know the Father, to insist that we know the Son, and then to ignore the Holy Spirit. After all, knowing the Spirit is the key to knowing the Father and the Son!

> **Fellowship is an incredibly dynamic activity. It involves communication, contribution co-operation, direction, action and accomplishment**

The Holy Spirit is the Spirit of fellowship. He is the Paraclete – the one like Jesus who is called alongside us. He comes alongside to create a relationship, a partnership, a fellowship.

It is a partnership with a clear common purpose: together, we – the Spirit and I, the Spirit and you – are going to do our utmost to bring great glory to Jesus in our bruised, broken and decadent world.

The fellowship of the Spirit is a life-long, intimate, personal relationship. We actually are living with him, living in him, existing in his presence. These are not nice religious phrases which sound good but mean nothing. They are to be taken at face value. The Holy Spirit wants to live with us, with each one of us – and that means exactly what it means in its everyday use in the world.

Of course, people find it difficult to imagine how we can

have a two-way live-in relationship with a spirit which involves listening, talking, walking, sharing and fellow-shipping. We have all seen concrete examples of fathers and sons so we can grasp the idea of a relationship with the Father and the Son. None of us, however, has a model on which we can base our fellowship with the Holy Spirit. Perhaps this is one reason why the church has neglected the Spirit.

It is vital that we return to a correct and biblical emphasis on the Spirit. There is no need to worry that we might give him too much attention, as all he talks about is Jesus. I guarantee that it is impossible to live with the Spirit and not be completely in love with Jesus. Remember, our fellowship with the Spirit has only one aim – to glorify Jesus.

DEVELOPING THE MINISTRY OF JESUS

We have seen that Jesus wants to continue his loving, healing, saving ministry to the world through us. And we know that he has given us the Holy Spirit so that we can have all the help we need to live his life, speak his words, and carry out his deeds.

God has created our partnership with the Spirit – our living in and with the Spirit – so that Jesus' ministry can continue. It is now our responsibility to develop our relationship with the Holy Spirit so that Jesus' ministry can become more effective in that small part of the world where we have been placed.

Discipleship

Living with the Spirit is fundamentally an issue of discipleship. Jesus' first partners in ministry were called 'disciples'. This means that the degree to which Jesus' ministry develops in us depends entirely on our commitment to discipleship. In fact, the whole of our Christian life should be discipleship – through and through!

1 John 2:6 states that 'Whoever claims to live in him must walk as Jesus did'. We need to follow Christ's example in everything – in our thinking and speaking, our living and praying, our compassion and serving, our ministry and our morality.

We need to know what Jesus thinks and how he responds to people. We need to understand his concerns and priorities. We need to absorb fully

Whoever claims to live in him must walk as Jesus did

his 'Sermon on the Mount' and really grasp his 'kingdom principles'. Then we need the help of the Spirit to implement rigorously the standards and pattern of Jesus' life and ministry into our own lives.

Discipleship means rejoicing when persecuted, initiating reconciliation, speaking simply, giving generously, loving enemies, living humbly, rejecting materialism, judging nobody. It means feeding the hungry, clothing the naked, visiting the imprisoned, welcoming foreigners, comforting the sick. It means obeying Jesus – doing our best not to presume or disobey.

When we live with the Spirit – exactly the same Holy Spirit who was with Jesus – we will hear the Spirit prompting us to think and act like Jesus. We will feel his quiet inner prompting to do this, to go there, to sit quietly, to be silent, to send a gift, to speak a brief sentence, and so on.

As it is a relationship, a fellowship, a partnership, the Spirit does not make us obey him. And as it is a committed relationship, the Spirit does not desert us when we act foolishly or sinfully. He is God with us, God alongside us – through thick and thin.

The degree of our commitment to the Spirit determines the level of our discipleship. If we are deadly serious about glorifying Jesus, we will depend entirely and exclusively on the Spirit and do out utmost to develop Christ's healing, saving ministry to the lost people around us.

'His' ministry

In 1 Corinthians 3:10-11, the apostle Paul makes it plain that the only valid ministry is Christ. 'By the grace God has given me, I laid a foundation as an expert builder, and someone else is building on it. But each one should be careful how he builds. For no one can lay any foundation other than the one already laid, which is Jesus Christ.'

Jesus' ministry is the only ministry. Anything else is fruitless self-assertion. Too many believers and leaders do things which seem to be good, that they hope God will bless. Too many people are concerned to publicise *their* activities, to advertise *their* ministries, to attract funds for what *they* are doing.

The repeated use of simple phrases like 'my ministry' or 'this ministry' give the game away. An over-emphasis on these things reveals an independent, ambitious attitude which fails to appreciate that there is only one ministry: and that is 'his ministry'.

The day I recognised that I had no ministry, and died to any thought of my own ministry, was the day when I received a share in Jesus' ministry.

I had been a Pentecostal minister for five years. I had

The day I recognised that I had no ministry, and died to any thought of my own ministry, was the day when I received a share in Jesus' ministry been baptized in the Holy Spirit. But I was still striving to establish 'my' ministry.

I was concerned with structures and traditions. Signs and wonders seemed to be an unattainable goal. Finally, I reached a point when I told the Lord that I was giving up. I said that I was a failure: I didn't have a ministry and would never have a ministry. At that point, in the quiet of my mind, the Lord seemed to say, 'I've been waiting to hear you say that. Now, are you ready to share my ministry?'

> The most significant decision you can make in the work of God's kingdom is to submit yourself to the Spirit's guidance and rule

It was clear that Jesus was asking me to die to any idea of my own ministry. I felt that he wanted me to empty myself of thoughts about ever having any ministry of my own. Somehow, he helped me to grasp that there was only one ministry – the ministry of the Holy Spirit, the ministry of Jesus Christ, the ministry of the Father.

I had to decide whether I was going to give up, or go on striving to establish myself, or submit myself to the direction and control of the Holy Spirit. It was my choice.

And I am sure that the most significant decision you can make in the work of the kingdom of God is whether you will submit yourself to the Spirit's guidance and rule.

The Spirit's guidance

The Spirit does not start guiding us when we submit to him. He has been at work, speaking quietly to us, right from the moment of regeneration. Obviously, we draw even closer to him when we are baptized in him by Jesus. We hear his prompting, but we do not necessarily recognise his voice or submit to it.

When I was a young Christian, I was involved in a drug rehabilitation work. One day I was due to speak about this work at a small church meeting. As I was praying at home before the meeting, I had a very funny feeling. I saw in my mind the face of a blind woman who was sitting in a particular place.

When the service began, the seat I had seen was empty. During the service, however, a blind woman came into the church and sat bang in the place I had visualised in prayer!

The Spirit was guiding me – though I didn't realise it was him and didn't know how to respond to his prompting.

My speaking at the service was rather immature. I made an appeal, and nobody responded. I felt that something should happen, and spoke to the woman after the service – asking her whether she knew that Jesus could heal. Yet, as I didn't know how to follow the Holy Spirit, the woman left the building as blind as she had entered it.

I know that very many believers have had similar experiences. We feel something inside us, and are not sure whether it is the Spirit's prompting, our natural hopes and aspirations, or devilish confusion. Sometimes we find ourselves suddenly focusing on a particular person; at other times we feel that we should say or do something. But we don't know what to do with these feelings.

If we are living in the Spirit's presence, we must expect him to guide and direct us with his gentle, quiet voice

Please remember, it is a *partnership*. The Holy Spirit does not compel us to obey him. He encourages. He advises. He may persist but he does not insist! Therefore it is critical that we learn to

> It is critical that we learn to recognise his voice, and to tell the difference between his prompting, our own ideas, and the devil's suggestions

recognise his voice, and to tell the difference between his prompting, our own ideas, and the devil's suggestions. We can only do this by acting on these inner promptings, by being ready to make mistakes and look foolish.

It has been so stressed in the church that prayers should be made to the Father, that many of us have found it difficult to develop an intimate relationship with the Spirit. Perhaps we think that he can speak to us but we can't speak to him.

As I developed as a Christian, I realised that I did not always need to pray on my knees, interceding and wrestling before the Father. Sometimes it seemed right for me to remain seated and to pray in a more conversational way with the Spirit. We cannot live in his presence and never communicate with him!

Once I had accepted that I would never have a ministry of my own, I was eager to be involved in the supernatural aspects of Jesus' ministry. But I could not find a context or framework for the miraculous.

I knew that the Spirit was trying to guide me, but I did not know what to do with his promptings. Eventually I became spiritually dry and stopped praying.

It was only when I came to Kensington Temple, and saw leaders like Wynne Lewis, Benson Idahosa and Charles and Paula Slagle, that I began to understand how the Spirit worked *with* us.

> I had been waiting for God to work *through* me. They showed me that God wanted to work *with* me

I had been expecting the Spirit somehow to control me and make things happen automatically. However, these godly leaders showed me that the Spirit would speak to me, and then I had to act on his words. I was a partner, not a puppet.

These prophetic men and women opened up Christ's supernatural ministry. I realised that everything hinged on my relationship with the Spirit. I needed to live so intimately with him that I could hear his quietest whisperings. I needed to submit so fully to him that I really did only do what he said. And I needed to depend entirely on his gifts and resources, rather than on my own training, experience, background and ideas.

They helped me to grasp that – as it was Christ's ministry – I had to follow his example in the gospels. I had to do nothing except what I saw the Father doing; say nothing except what I heard the Spirit saying; go nowhere except where I saw the Father leading.

During the last ten years, I have slowly begun to recognise the Spirit's promptings and to trust him more and more. I have learnt – through many mistakes and disappointments – how important it is to wait for the Spirit, instead of dashing ahead in human enthusiasm or because of people's expectations.

Whenever it seems that I am prompted to minister – whether in public or private, at a meeting or in the street – I find that there are three critical questions which I need to answer. Am I hearing the Spirit correctly? Have I the faith and courage to rise to the challenge? Am I brave enough to wait for the Spirit and not to fake anything?

> Am I hearing the Spirit correctly? Have I the faith to rise to the challenge? Am I courageous enough to wait for the Spirit and not to fake anything?

When I am doing normal everyday things like travelling and shopping, the greatest temptation for me is to do nothing. If I hear the Spirit prompting me to speak a quiet word to a stranger, I soon hear the enemy urging me not to make a fool of myself, not to embarrass the person, not to risk making a mistake.

And when I am speaking at a large meeting, the enemy puts pressure on me not to disappoint the people who want a good show! I have been tempted to speak vague and general words rather than to wait for the Spirit's specific word for a particular person.

DEPENDING ON THE SPIRIT

At the start of this book we thought about the massive needs of the world – of people we know personally, and of those we hear about in the media. Please recognise that we all feel impotent in the face of such great needs. And that is exactly how it should be!

If we are concerned to develop Christ's ministry to lost people, we need to develop the awareness he had that we can do nothing on our own.

We live in an age when there is tremendous pressure on us to appear competent and successful. Yet we will only make spiritual progress when we fully grasp that we can't do anything on our own.

> We will make spiritual progress only when we fully grasp that we can't do anything on our own

We have been made for a relationship with God, and we experience that on earth in fellowship with the Spirit. It is only by depending on the Spirit that we can begin to minister in the Spirit.

In 1 Kings 18, Elijah faced the prophets of Baal on Mount Carmel. Please read the chapter and note the contrast between a Spirit-filled true prophet and false prophets.

Elijah did not try to make anything happen. He did not strike a spark and ask the people to believe that this was the fire of God. In fact, he did everything possible to prove to the people that he was not the cause of the miracle.

Instead of putting fire under the sacrifice, he poured gallons of water over it. As far as he was concerned, it had to be God or nothing. By his words and actions, Elijah ensured that nobody could think he had been anything more than God's mouthpiece.

God or nothing

Back in the early-eighties when I was spiritually dry, I was rather judgmental of the men and women I saw involved in 'signs and wonders' ministries. I was not impressed by what they claimed as miracles: so much seemed to be fleshly self-effort. I thought that they were trying to 'pump things up'.

However, God rebuked me through an elderly woman. I had watched her be grabbed from a wheelchair, and all she could manage after her 'miracle' was to totter feebly.

I spoke to her after the meeting, and she was radiant. She was so happy to have more movement and comfort than she had known in years. Even though she did not walk freely until later, I know that she never returned to her wheelchair.

God used this lady to deal with my judgmental attitude, but I have been determined to try and ensure that what we do in ministry does not make it easy for people to be cynical.

Like Elijah, we need to make it hard for watching people to think that what happens is due to manipulation or pressure. It has to be God or nothing.

> Like Elijah, we need to make it as hard as possible for watching people to think that what happens is due to manipulation or pressure

We can see this in Jesus' ministry. When we read the gospels we see that he either went directly to specific individuals or responded to particular requests.

For example, in John 5, although there was 'a great multitude of sick people, blind, lame and paralysed' Jesus only ministered to 'a certain man'. He did not make a general appeal for sick people who wanted healing to identify themselves. He did not offer healing prayer to the crowds. Instead, he listened to the Spirit and was led directly to the one person whom God was dealing with.

Many today would be tempted by the crowds of sick people to make only a vague, general appeal for healing – rather than a Spirit-directed word to only one person. But a general appeal was not God's will on this occasion. It must be God or nothing. If we are to share in Christ's ministry, we need always to listen carefully to the Spirit to ensure that we do not say or do things because of pressure and expectations.

No exaggeration

One of the most extraordinary features of Jesus' ministry is the way that he often asked people who had been healed to tell *nobody* about the miracle. Mark 7:31-37 and 8:22-26 reveal this holy desire to work unobtrusively – which is one of the hallmarks of the humble, self-effacing Spirit.

Jesus did not use the people who had been healed just as a means to publicise his ministry. He did not press them to testify in an attempt to attract more people to listen to his message. He never tried to impress people by exaggerating what had taken place.

> When we depend on the Spirit, we will not feel the need to use worldly methods of self-publicity

We must be careful that we

do not make false claims, that we never overstate events, and that we do not use words like 'the best' and 'the greatest' which – frankly – are rarely, if ever, true. And we must also watch that we don't understate what God is doing in an attempt to appear humble. Both are equally wrong.

If we are serious about depending on the Spirit of truth, about sharing in Christ's unpretentious ministry, we will be characterised by holy humility and simple, straightforward speech. When we deeply depend on the Spirit, we will not feel the need to use worldly methods of self-publicity which overstate facts, ignore mistakes, and focus attention in entirely the wrong direction.

The Spirit's anointing

Depending on the Spirit means relying on our anointing with him by Jesus. This is where developing Christ's ministry and depending on the Spirit draw together, for Jesus is the Baptizer: anointing us with the Spirit is an important part of his ministry.

People are sometimes confused today by the phrase 'anointing' as it is used to describe a wide variety of spiritual experiences.

In the Old Testament, priests, judges and kings were normally anointed once in a brief ceremony. However, their status as 'anointed' continued for the rest of their lives. The word 'anointing' describes both the moment when they were anointed and their ongoing spiritual condition.

> The word 'anointing' describes both the moment when they were anointed, and their ongoing spiritual condition

Jesus was always the Anointed One – the Christ, the Messiah – but there was also a moment in time at the Jordan when he was anointed by the Father with the Spirit.

129

The disciples received power and enabling when the Spirit came upon them at Pentecost, and they remained anointed from that moment onwards.

So it is with us. There is a moment of *initial anointing* when Jesus baptizes us in the Spirit. There is a *continual anointing* which describes our state as believers who are living in and with the Spirit. Then there are moments of *special anointing* when God, by the Spirit, equips us in a special way for a particular need, office or aspect of ministry.

For example, my *initial anointing* took place when I was baptized in the Spirit. I was eighteen years old and had been a Christian for two months. However, I was soon drawn off course, I became spiritually dry and did not depend on the anointing that God had given me.

Then, in 1985, Benson Idahosa was led by God to lay hands on me to receive a *special anointing* in the area of signs and wonders. I had been anointed with the Spirit when I was eighteen, but this seems to have been the first in a series of anointings for particular purposes – rather like Paul describes in 2 Timothy 1:6.

Since that time, although *continually anointed*, there have been a few occasions when God has seemed to be with me in a quite special way. Living with the Spirit means an unpredictable existence. Remember, he is a holy hurricane who blows where he will, not a tame God who does what we expect. When we are in fellowship with him, we must expect periods of calm interrupted by moments of extraordinary activity.

Of course, a special anointing does not mean that we can

Living with the Spirit means an unpredictable existence. Remember, he is a holy hurricane who blows where he will, not a tame God who does what we expect

function independently of God. An anointing in healing does not mean that we should visit as many hospitals as we can, laying hands on all the people in every ward!

Some people seem to forget that anointing equips us to do only what the Spirit directs. Remember, we are anointed with the Spirit *himself* not with a particular ability. This means that we must remain in him – in step with him – for the anointing to be effective. We cannot wander off and do our own thing just because we've been anointed!

When we read the New Testament, we can see that the disciples' anointing took place in Acts 2:4. They were immersed in the Spirit by Jesus, with all the consequences we have examined.

However, there were times when they were particularly anointed with the Spirit to fulfil a specific purpose. For example, Acts 4:7-8 describes how Peter was specially filled with the Spirit to speak to the Sanhedrin.

Some people explain these instances with a word-picture of 'leaky vessels'. They suggest that we are buckets full of holes who constantly leak the Spirit away and need to be repeatedly topped up. We have seen that plunging a sponge into a bucket is a more accurate picture of spiritual filling.

Once we are placed in the Spirit by Jesus we remain in the Spirit. We go on living in the anointing, which means that – as Ephesians 5:18 suggests – we go on being filled. But there can be special 'outpourings' for particular needs.

> Why were there unusual miracles in Ephesus and not in Corinth?

Just as there can be a sudden torrential downpour on a rainy day, so life in the breeze of the Spirit is punctuated by those moments when he blows with special and unusual power.

Acts 18 describes a period of about two years in Paul's life. It shows that he worked in Corinth as a tentmaker, held debates in the synagogues, founded a church, and then travelled through Galatia. Of course, Paul was anointed all this time. He was in and with the Spirit. But there are no records of any miracles.

Yet when Paul moved on to Ephesus – where he stayed for another two years – Acts 19:11 comments that 'God worked unusual miracles by the hands of Paul'. Why were there unusual miracles in Ephesus and not in Corinth? Why, when Paul moved on to Caesarea for two years, are there no records of any miracles there either?

We either conclude that Paul had leaked so much of the anointing away in Corinth and Caesarea that the Spirit could not work through him. Or the more likely explanation is that Paul had a special anointing in Ephesus because unusual miracles were on the Spirit's agenda for the town at that time.

DISCERNING THE SPIRIT'S AGENDA

It seems to me that one of the most basic ministry principles is this: God does not give power for what he is not doing, but he always provides power for what he is doing.

Some people appear to think that God gives us unlimited power, and that – once we have received his power – we should be able to minister powerfully whenever and wherever we are.

> God does not give power for what he is not doing, but he always provides power for what he is doing

Yet Jesus, who was fully God and – as a man – had received the Spirit without measure, appears not to

132

have healed everyone and definitely did not raise everyone from the dead.

The gospels suggest that Jesus healed all those who were brought to him, and that he took God's healing directly to specific individuals – ignoring crowds of other sick people around them. Clearly, he only did what the Father was doing – he stuck rigidly to the Spirit's agenda.

We are doomed to disappointment and embarrassing failure if we try to take the initiative in ministry or follow our own inclination. It is imperative that we wait for the Holy Spirit and receive specific directions and revelation from him before we proceed in active ministry.

Waiting

Most believers find that knowing God's will is one of the hardest parts of the Christian life. Our problem is not so much obeying God as knowing what to obey.

We long to obey him. We know that is the best and right thing to do. But we don't always know what | **Our problem is recognising his voice when we hear it**

he wants us to do. Instead of waiting for direction, we presume and flounder around, doing whatever seems to be best.

In John 10:16, 27, Jesus promised that his sheep would hear his voice. This is a promise which he has kept. By the Spirit, we do hear Christ's voice. The problem is that most of us don't recognise his voice when we hear it.

Sometimes we hear his voice, but are not sure whether it really is his voice – or our own thoughts or demonic temptations. At other times, our minds are so full of clutter and distractions that we cannot hear his voice clearly. We know that he is speaking to us, but we cannot make out what he is saying.

I have found that – for me – it is vital to spend time waiting on God before I begin listening to God. I need to make sure that I am alone and free from all possible distractions.

Ideally, I try to ensure that I still myself by quietly reading the scriptures for about an hour. Next, I spend time dealing with my feelings of anxiety and worthlessness – allowing the love of God to drive out all my fears. Only then am I ready to 'tune in to the Spirit' and receive his directions.

If I start asking the Spirit questions too soon, my mind is too busy and noisy to hear his quiet replies. I have found that I need to wait patiently on God – creating an oasis of peace in my life through meditating on his word – before I start listening for the Spirit's direction.

Listening

I expect that we all need to spend more time in listening prayer than we do. Too often our prayers are one way. We spend time asking God to do things, rather than asking him what we should do – and then listening for his reply.

> Asking God specific questions is a good way of learning to identify God's voice

Asking God specific questions is often a good way of learning to identify God's voice. Please don't be frightened to ask God what you should do or say. But remember to make sure that you take note of any thoughts which come into your mind. Then put those thought into practice and see what happens!

We will only learn to recognise God's quiet voice by acting on what we hear in our inner spirit. Some people are so worried about doing something wrong that they never do anything! Whereas others are so confident that every crazy thought is a divine instruction that they say and do ridiculous things. This means that we need to develop discernment when we listen for God's answers to our questions.

God does not promise us sensational results if we do what he says. He does not try to persuade us to do something by telling us what our obedience will achieve. That is a human way of thinking.

Equally, God never asks us to do something which is contrary to Scripture, or which is destructive or lacking in love. Instead, his thoughts always encourage, build up, mend, comfort and so on.

When God instructs us, he simply tells us what to do – without any reasons or explanations – because he wants to develop our faith and trust. Then he gently persists with that thought over a period of time.

In listening prayer, we should ensure that we intercede for boldness along the lines of Acts 4:29-30, as well as asking about the who, how, when, where and what of ministry.

As time goes by, we will begin to recognise the Spirit's special way of speaking to us. We should never stop spending time alone with him to develop our relationship. However, we will increasingly recognise his way of interrupting our thoughts when he wants us to speak to a particular person. I have found that some of the most precious times of ministry have occurred when I have trusted these sudden, unsought thoughts.

> In listening prayer, we should ensure that we intercede for boldness, as well as asking about the who, where, when, how and what of ministry

Sometimes it is easy. At an airport transfer desk, I

suddenly 'knew' that the officer was a brother in Christ. I don't know how I knew, the Spirit just popped the thought into my mind.

I might have looked foolish if I had been wrong, but we had a lovely conversation which was listened to avidly by the two neighbouring officials – who were deeply involved with other religions. I didn't have to do anything difficult – I merely had to act on what I heard.

Another time, I was convinced that the Spirit wanted me to say something to my dentist. I was very embarrassed as I lay in the chair and didn't dare speak – so God arranged that I needed to return in a few days for further treatment! I spent time at home quietly asking God what to say and asking for boldness. It wasn't anything too hard, just a simple message of comfort about a sick relative.

> Too many believers ignore the 'everyday' thoughts which the Spirit places in their minds

God is concerned about every aspect of our lives. Too many believers think that 'ministry' means nothing but miracles, so they ignore the 'everyday' thoughts which the Spirit places in our minds. Living in fellowship with the Spirit means being ready to be involved in anything on his agenda – small, unseen words and deeds of comfort, as well as more public signs and wonders.

Asking

Jesus' initiative for ministry was either someone asking him for help or God directing him to a particular needy person.

Many of us still find it hard to hear God's precise direction, and tend to offer a general description which may fit several people. But we must press on, and pray that we will know specifically who and what is on God's agenda.

When we actually are ministering to a person, we need to listen to both God and the person we are helping. This is helped by creating a climate of quiet and privacy. Time and again, Jesus silenced noise or moved into a private place before commencing ministry.

As well as functioning supernaturally, Jesus also worked at the natural level of observation and deduction. He asked normal and natural questions which helped in ministry. If he needed to ask the questions in Mark 5:9; 8:23; 9:21; Luke 18:41 & John 5:6, so will we.

'What is your name?' The exchange of names is more than mere politeness. It helps to ensure that our ministry is personal and loving.

'What do you want God to do?' This helps the person to be specific in their request.

'Do you want to be well?' We need to check that the person is serious about ministry, willing to be healed, and aware of the likely consequences of God's work in their life.

'How long has this been happening?' Sometimes we need to talk about the background to grasp the cause of the problem.

'Can you see?' We always need to check whether anything has happened during our ministry. It is irresponsible to pass from person to person without checking what God has done.

As well as asking the person questions, we always need to ask God whether anything else needs to be known. We should ask God to show us what is happening, what caused the problem, what he wants us to do, and so on.

> We should ask God to show us what is happening, what caused the problem, what he wants us to do

The Spirit may give us a picture or word to pass on,

suggest a statement we should make, or put a question into our mind. The cause of the problem is often self-evident, but sometimes we need God to reveal whether it is physical, emotional, spiritual, demonic, hereditary or a curse. If God tells us nothing, we know all we need to know.

We need to watch that we don't slip into the trap of assuming that every problem is caused by sin, or by a demon, or by childhood problems – and so on.

Sin sometimes is the cause of the problem. A demon may have to be ejected. A curse may have to be broken. The sins of the parents may need to be forgiven. But we cannot ever dare assume that we know the solution just because we know the problem. There is no prepared grid which sets out the solution for every different problem.

We have to depend on the Spirit. We must listen to his instructions. If we catch ourselves only saying and doing the same things that we've said and done before, there's a good chance we are depending on experience rather than the Spirit!

There is no prepared grid which sets out the solution for every different problem

Once we have asked all the relevant questions, we don't look in a book for the appropriate ministry. We turn to our partner, the Holy Spirit, for our directions.

Understanding

The description of the Spirit in Isaiah 11:2 helps us to appreciate the way he equips us. It lists six attributes of the Spirit which have particular application when we are ministering. He is: 'The Spirit of wisdom and understanding. The Spirit of counsel and might. The Spirit of knowledge and of the fear of the Lord.'

These are not gifts which are occasionally given, but the very essence of the Spirit's being. They naturally flow from him to those who live in and with him. We do not have to sweat, pray or wait for them. If we have received him, we will receive them quite naturally. They are more like the fruit of the Spirit than the gifts of the Spirit.

He is the Spirit of wisdom or skill. I believe that this is the supernatural ability to know what to do or say next.

He is the Spirit of understanding or insight. This reveals the real problem which lies behind the words of the needy person we are helping. We do not need to have experienced their problem to have insight into it.

He is the Spirit of counsel or advice. This is the Spirit-given provision of the words to speak. We often wonder what we can possibly say to a person when a sudden thought flashes through our minds. This is the Spirit of counsel at work. It is the utterance of an inspired sentence which brings the solution one step nearer.

He is the Spirit of might or authority. This is the authority of God which is added to our words by the Spirit. A sentence may be spoken in fear and hesitation but received as a blinding revelation. This is the work of the Spirit.

He is the Spirit of knowledge of facts. God may suggest a key fact to us which unlocks the puzzle, but we will need wisdom as to how we mention this.

And he is the Spirit of the fear or reverence of the Lord. When we are ministering, we should be more fearful of what God will think if we do not pass on his words than of what the person will say if we do. God's foolishness is much greater than our wisdom, and only when we have a right and healthy fear of God will we be ready to pass on his words.

These attributes should not be surrounded by such a glow

> These attributes should not be surrounded by such a glow that we think they can be experienced only rarely

that we think they can only be rarely experienced. We should not have a false *super*-supernatural approach to the Spirit which stops us manifesting his attributes.

We do not create or perform gifts or attributes, we make room for God to give them. They are not abilities to do something, but the work of the Lord Jesus through us. They are the energy of the Spirit, not human activity. We don't dig into our personal resources for understanding, instead we should pass on what we have received at that moment from our partner, the Holy Spirit. He provides us with all the understanding we need to minister effectively.

DEMONSTRATIONS OF THE SPIRIT

When we are living in and with the Spirit, we share his calling to glorify Jesus. Whether good or flawed, everything we do and say is some sort of witness to Jesus. By now, we should know that the Spirit longs to fill us with his power and purity so that every aspect of our lives will bring much greater glory to the Son.

We also know that we are Christ's body on earth. We are his hands, feet and voice. In fellowship with the Spirit and each other, we share in Christ's ministry to the needy around us. This is a high responsibility which we must take seriously. It means that we should always be ready to minister,

> **Most of the time we will be directed to minister while we are out and about in everyday life**

always be paying attention to the Holy Spirit so that we stick tight to his agenda.

Sometimes we will be called to minister in a meeting – like Jesus in the synagogue, and Paul at the breaking of bread in Troas. But most of the time we will be directed to minister while we are out and about in everyday life.

Most people were healed by Jesus when he was on a

140

journey. Others were healed by him in their beds, in a garden, at a funeral, at a meal and so on. It was the same in the early church. People were healed in the street, on the way to a prayer meeting, in private homes, out in the countryside, and at an open-air evangelistic rally.

One of the reasons why we have struggled with signs and wonders is that we have concentrated too much on ministry in meetings. God seems to delight in healing at the roadside, in healing in the course of daily living, in healing social outcasts who will never attend a church meeting. We should remember this if we want to share in the 'greater things' promised by Jesus.

Obviously I am seen to be involved in a great deal of public ministry in meetings, but that is by far the smaller part of my ministry. Our congregations have grown and multiplied only because all of our members have started to share in Christ's ministry – seven days a week, wherever they live and work.

> God delights in healing at the roadside, in healing in the course of daily living, in healing social outcasts who will never attend a meeting

We are now going to look at what we do when we minister. But please, don't think only about meetings and services when you read this. I am offering principles which apply wherever and whenever the Spirit prompts you to speak and act – whether in a supermarket or office, a bus or back garden, a private home or even the dentist's.

Prayer

The first scriptural healing story shows the importance of prayer. Genesis 20:17 reports that 'Abraham prayed to God; and God healed Abimelech, his wife, and his maidservants'. 1 Kings 13:6, 17:20-22; 2 Kings 4:33-36 & 20:5 underline the fact that prayer is a vital part of ministry.

In the New Testament, when Peter arrived at Tabitha's house in Jaffa, Acts 9:40 shows that he 'knelt down and prayed'. We don't know exactly what he prayed, but we know what happened when he had finished praying!

It appears that there are four aspects of prayer in ministry. We will always need to pray, though not necessarily audibly, however we will need the Spirit's guidance as to the type and content of our praying.

In John 14:12-14 Jesus makes one of his greatest promises. 'He who believes in me, the works that I do he will do also; and greater works than these he will do, because I go to my Father. And whatever you ask in my name, that I will do, that the Father may be glorified in the Son. If you ask anything in my name, I will do it.'

There is a similar promise in John 16:24. In ministry, we do well to start by claiming these promises, and by making brief *petitions* which ask God to do what we understand to be on the Spirit's agenda.

Sometimes we don't know what to pray. Romans 8:26-27 promises that the Spirit helps us by making *intercessions* according to the will of God.

> We are not on our own – we have a partner who is interceding for us!

We are not on our own – we have a partner who is interceding for us! Personally, I find it helpful to pray silently in tongues when I am not sure how to proceed. At times it is right to suspend ministry for a few days so that we can have a prolonged time of intercession before continuing.

Prayers of *pronouncement* feature very strongly in the New Testament accounts of ministry. Time and again, Jesus commanded 'Be cleansed', 'Arise', 'Stretch out your arm', and so on. Peter ordered 'In the name of Jesus Christ, walk. Ananias announced, 'I have been sent by the Lord Jesus so that you may recover your sight'. Peter said, 'Jesus Christ cures you: get up'. And Paul shouted 'Get to your feet – stand up' (Acts 3:16; 9:17, 34; 14:10).

James 5:15 suggests that 'the prayer of *faith* will save the sick, and the Lord will raise him up'. It appears that this describes a special impartation of faith which is given for that moment. We won't always experience this!

Many times we pray because we have been asked or prompted and have little expectation of anything happening. Yet, now and again, God overwhelms us with his faith and we pray just like Jesus described in Mark 11:24.

Gifts

1 Corinthians 12:4-11 is a key passage about spiritual gifts. The Greek word for 'give' in 12:7 suggests that God's giving of gifts to each believer is an on-going activity and not a once-for-all action.

This means that we don't receive gifts as personal possessions, but that we are given whatever gift we need when we need it. Instead of endlessly asking 'what is my gift?', we would be better to go on asking God to equip us with whatever we need for the task in hand.

The gospels show Jesus using all the gifts of the Spirit in ministry, except tongues and interpretation, and we can expect to do the same. We don't need to worry about defining the gifts too carefully, as the New Testament does not do this, rather it encourages us to use them. Remember, they are

> We don't receive gifts as personal possessions, we are given whatever gift we need whenever we need it

tools for practical use, not toys for amusement or trophies which reward performance.

Although undefined, the gifts are self-explanatory – knowledge of facts, wisdom for guidance, faith to act, prophecy for speech, discernment to distinguish between spirits, healing and miracles to bring a supernatural change. In ministry, we need to rely on our partner the Spirit to provide the gifts we need, then we should trust the thoughts he gives and act on them.

Obviously we will make mistakes. The disciples failed Jesus in Mark 9:14-29, and we will fail him too – we are not as fully developed as Jesus was. But I promise that you will develop more skill in manifesting the gifts if you persevere through the inevitable failures and errors.

Faith

Some believers think that they need huge amounts of faith for ministry, whereas Jesus suggested that we need only a tiny amount of genuine faith – the size of a mustard seed.

Others seem to believe that human faith is what makes miracles happen, when – of course – it is God's power.

Faith has been called 'believing God and acting on it'. It is the logic of God's capability when it comes to doing what he has promised to do.

Faith is like the clutch in a car. There might be a powerful engine roaring under the bonnet, but the car remains stationery until the driver presses the clutch and slips the gear. The clutch does not make the car move, it merely engages the power.

Faith is believing God and acting on it

If we have a choice between two cars, one brand new and the other an old wreck, we don't need much faith to believe that the new car will take us to our destination. So it is almost an insult to suggest that we need much faith in our God to believe that he can work a miracle.

Matthew 9:2, 22, 29 & Mark 6:1-6 show that we do need faith in ministry. But not a spine-tingling faith which brings us out in goose-bumps, just enough belief to engage the power. We simply need to believe that God can do what is needed, and to be ready to act as his hands and his voice.

Sometimes God will give us a special gift of faith when he wants to do something remarkable: he does this by adding his faith to ours. More commonly, our simple confident belief in God is all the faith we need.

Action

When we are ministering to needy people, the Spirit guides along his own creative path. He might prompt us to do something unusual – like Jesus anointing a man's eyes with saliva. But this doesn't mean that we should ever do the same thing again unless he clearly instructs us; and if he's not doing it, neither can we.

However, I think that there are several basic, common-sense principles which seem to make sense in most settings.

We should show Christ's love. Smile, use first names, and relax. After all, God performs the miracle, not us; and if he's not doing it, neither can we.

We ask the Holy Spirit to provide us with guidance, boldness, power and purity. We keep our eyes open at all times. Some information is received only by watching how the person responds to God's power.

> Show Christ's love at all times. Smile, use first names, and relax. God performs the miracle, not us

We should listen attentively to God and speak whatever he puts into our mind. He may tell us to command a growth to be removed or an organ to be restored. He may ask us to announce faith, freedom or blessing. He might ask us to squeeze the person's hand and remain silent. We should ask God whether it is right to touch the person or not. If it seems best, we can gently place our hands on the clothing nearest to the affected part of the body.

We should ask the person, 'Do you feel anything?' 'What is happening?' We need to ensure that they keep us informed about the healing progress – or lack of it!

We watch for bodily reactions to the Spirit's work. The person may shake, stiffen, sag or fall. Their breathing may change rapidly. They might tingle, laugh or cry. Their eyes may moisten. They might feel strangely hot – and so on.

Although these reactions often indicate that God is at work, they are only the body's reaction to God's power. A strong physical reaction does not evidence a greater work, nor does the absence of any bodily reaction mean nothing is happening in the spiritual realm.

Fifty sunbathers lying on a beach all have slightly different bodily reactions to the sun's power. It is the same when the Spirit moves in power. A few always fall over. Some are bound to shake. Many people, as in the gospel accounts, evidence nothing.

> Although these reactions indicate that God is at work, they are only the body's reaction to God's power

If a bodily reaction does takes place, we should help the person to be as comfortable as possible. But we usually need to ignore the reaction and press on with the ministry.

We should continually encourage and relax the person we are helping. We can remind them of God's power, presence and promises. It might be helpful to suggest that they read a particular Scripture passage.

We can silently use the gift of tongues, and should stop ministering when the Spirit's agenda has been achieved, or when we can't think of anything else to say or do, or when the person asks us to stop, or when anyone seems tired. If God's objective has clearly not been attained, we should arrange to minister again in the near future – allowing time to elapse for further preparation, prayer and fasting.

Humility

Many people are attracted to ministry – especially healing – for wrong reasons. Compassion and obedience are all that motivated Christ.

We will have been side-tracked if we hope to stare at miracles or be entertained by bodily reactions. And we will have been diverted if we plan to send out insensitive press reports on what has happened among *us* at *our* meetings.

We should seek the holy anonymity of the Spirit and aim to rivet attention on God alone, without basking in any associated glory.

No man or woman can work a miracle. No human can heal another. The highest we can aim is to be an unprofitable servant whom

> The Spirit is the floodlight; our words and actions are the rays of light. Jesus is illuminated and glorified

God tips off a few minutes in advance of a miracle. We are lowly couriers, not the manufacturer. Holy humility is much easier when we have grasped this simple fact.

The Spirit's work is to glorify Jesus. We are called to partner him in his work. When a building is floodlit, it is the building which is admired: the floodlights and rays are necessary, but unnoticed.

In ministry, the Holy Spirit is the floodlight; our words and actions are the rays of light energized by the Spirit. Jesus is Illuminated and glorified. He must be noticed, not us. He is to be admired, not the mighty deeds or bodily reactions.

Obvious and unassumed humility is a key demonstration of the character of the Spirit. Just as we need power and purity, so humility must accompany signs and wonders.

DISCIPLESHIP WITH THE SPIRIT

In Luke 17:15-19, John 5:14 & 9:35-38 we see how Jesus followed through after ministry with people he had helped.

He returned to the man he had healed at the pool and told him not to sin any more. When Jesus heard that the blind man had been banned from the synagogue, he sought him out to bring him some spiritual comfort and to lead him to the Messiah. And he added a spiritual blessing to the physical healing of the leper who had returned to him with praise and thanksgiving.

People often do not receive everything from God when we minister to them for the first time. We may need to go back to them several times to help them receive whatever God has for them.

When we are thinking about what has happened, the Spirit frequently puts a thought into our minds and we wish that we had said this or done that. It is often right to go back to the person and briefly mention this 'afterthought' – just as Jesus returned to the man in John 5:14.

Jesus followed through after ministry with people he had helped

If we share in Jesus' ministry to the people we meet while travelling, it will sometimes be impossible to meet people a second or third time.

We need to recognise that God often uses us as one small link in a long chain of his servants. However, we should go on praying for the people we have helped even if we cannot meet them again.

After ministry

When, in partnership with the Spirit, we have finished ministering to someone we need to ask our partner what we should do next.

It may be right to say and do nothing except pray. But – if the ministry has been extended and we have sought God for healing, freedom or

> Explain the Good News to them, and point them towards the next step in Christian commitment

special direction – it is usually good to encourage the person to offer praise and thanksgiving.

When we have prayed for healing, and the person has been receiving special medical care or using prescribed drugs, we should encourage the person to visit their doctor. This seems to have been Jesus' concern in Matthew 8:4.

If we are living with the Spirit and eager to develop Jesus' ministry, most of the people we minister to will be *unbelievers*. It is good to explain the Good News to them, and point them towards the next step in Christian commitment, whether repentance, baptism, receiving the Spirit, or joining a local congregation

It is helpful to sit down a few days after ministering and to go through what happened. We can learn much from our mistakes if we are prepared to acknowledge them. There will be moments when we will have been too timid and others when we will have been too forceful. We should reflect honestly on what happened and ask the Spirit to show us where we were out-of-step with him.

Most importantly, we must recognise that we may have a God-given responsibility for the person we have met. Obviously we will pray for their safety and spiritual development, but we will need the Spirit's guidance as to whether we should become more closely involved.

We know that the Spirit has come alongside us to encourage, comfort, teach and direct us. When we are living in him, we will naturally be led alongside people to help and encourage them in a similar way.

The great teaching about spiritual gifts in 1 Corinthians 12 – 14 is set in the context of teaching about building up the body of Christ and building it together. This means that the way we help people through the gifts should not be isolated from the body.

When we are involved with people in ministry, we will want to achieve whatever is on the Spirit's agenda. But we know that – whatever else we do – the Spirit will want us to introduce the person to the presence of God. We cannot do this on our own – we can only do this in relationship with other believers.

> When we are living in the Spirit, we will be led alongside people to help and encourage them

Corporate ministry

The principle of partnership runs through the Bible. One solitary individual cannot reflect the image of the triune God; it needs a relationship. The promises of Matthew 18:19-20 are made to two or three, not to one. Jesus sent his followers out to minister in pairs, not on their own. Protection from the enemy forces is granted to the church, not to isolated individuals – and so on.

Matthew 10:1-16 shows how Jesus sent the Twelve to

minister in partnership, and Luke 10:1-20 describes how seventy-two others were sent in the same way.

This does not mean that we refuse to minister if nobody else is with us. The book of Acts contains many examples of believers who were sent by the Spirit to minister on their own – for example, Philip in Acts 8:26-40 and Ananias in Acts 9:10-19. But Philip was one of the Seven, the apostles worked mainly in pairs, and Paul always ministered with close companions.

The disciples learnt from being with Jesus when he ministered, and it

There are many advantages when we minister in pairs

is good preparation for us to join with other more experienced believers. This is one way to multiply the numbers of believers who are actively involved in ministry.

There are many advantages when we minister is pairs: an increase in power; more channels for God to use in communication; and more protection from foolish mistakes. Faith is maintained more easily; different gifts and abilities complement each other; courage exists that one person never has; and the flow of ministry can pass from one to another. One person is precluded from claiming God's work as their personal achievement, and the inevitable mistakes cannot be hidden.

When we are ministering in such a vital partnership, it is easier to lead the people we have helped into similar corporate relationships. For most of this century, the church's evangelism has concentrated on personal salvation – on an individual's vertical relationship with God.

More recently, the Spirit of truth has shown us that our horizontal relationships with other believers are equally important. Our ministry must build the people we help into a corporate life which reflects the dynamic relationship of the Triune God.

Acts 2:41 does not record that three thousand were converted, it states that they were 'added to them'. Their salvation had an essential corporate dynamic. They were not saved to go back to their old lives, they were saved to join a new community.

The signs and wonders ministry described in Acts 2:43 is surrounded by a wonderful description of the redeemed community's life. On through Acts, it is not possible to imagine ministry apart from the Christian community. When the Holy Spirit led New Testament believers to needy people, they brought them into the church.

> The Spirit wants to knit us together in dynamic communities which are full of the presence of God

So, when we have ministered to people today, we must encourage them to become part of a living, loving local congregation. Although this book has mainly focused on the Spirit's work in individual believers, we must realise that the Spirit wants to knit us together in dynamic communities which are full of the presence of God.

Community Life

We are our brother's keeper. We dare not be casual with the people whom God has guided us to help. Some leaders may be gifted and appointed to pastoral care, but this is also the responsibility of every believer.

We are called to care for each other in a loving, forgiving and practical way which shows that we are the Lord's. It is not enough to arrange and attend powerful mid-week meetings and wonderful Sunday services if there is no day-in, day-out community life which draws people to Jesus – the head of the church.

The Spirit is the witness to Jesus. He pours power and

purity into our lives so that we become ever more accurate witnesses to the character of Jesus. But he also is working to bring us *together* under Christ.

Please read Ephesians 1:3-23 and grasp the extent to which we are called together. Soak up Ephesians 2 and realise that it about 'us together'.

We are 'fellow citizens with the saints and members of the household of God'. We are 'joined together'. We are growing 'into a holy temple in the Lord'. We are 'being built together for a habitation of God in the Spirit'.

Sometimes it seems easier just to get on with the job on our own – working at relationships can be such hard work. Yet Jesus submitted to and depended on people in a quite striking way.

He meekly submitted to his parents, to John's baptism, to the synagogue authorities, to political leaders, to Jewish priests, to Pilate. If we want to live and minister with his authority, we need to live as he lived – voluntarily under the authority of others.

Jesus accepted the service of those who accompanied him. He stayed with people who wanted to look after him.

> We are being built *together* for a habitation of God in the Spirit

He valued the company of the disciples. He needed Simon to carry his cross for him. If we want to give we must be willing to receive. If we want to minister we must be able to accept help and show that we depend on others. We do all this in the church – that wonderful community which is meant to show the Christ-life to the world.

We have been rescued from sin to be part of a healing community, a loving community, a community which is throbbing with the life of the Holy Spirit, a community which is constantly reaching out to the people round about. We should be doing everything possible to develop such a community and to draw the people we help into the Spirit's common life.

Together in the Spirit, we have been equipped to exercise authority over all evil powers in our area. In the name of Jesus and in the power of the Spirit, the congregations I lead in London are going out into the darkness and are helping people to renounce their involvement in evil practices and turn to Jesus.

Together with the Spirit we are being inspired to discover a life of service which follows Christ's sacrificial, foot-washing example. We share his authority to reach out in his name with healing to the sick and broken-hearted around us. We are starting to lay down our lives in the service of believers and unbelievers alike.

Together in the Spirit, we are living a life which is slowly moving towards Christ's perfection. With his help, we are beginning to understand our neighbours with the insight and sympathy of Christ. We are getting closer to those with whom we have little in common. We are taking God's comfort and encouragement where it is needed most.

And together, in and with the Spirit, we are learning to radiate God's love, to shine with his light and truth, to display more and more of his glory. We are making God's presence felt in our streets in deeply practical ways – but only because we are partners with the Spirit in his work, because we are beginning to live in the presence of God.

CONCLUSION

This book has been based in real life. It is not a collection of nice ideas which have been developed while we have been sitting around in armchairs. Instead, the material has grown out of the lives of hundreds of ordinary people who have worked and worshipped with me in London, especially during the last ten years.

In the churches I lead, we are surrounded by desperate need, by people whose lives are in tatters, by whole communities under stress. For years we have ached to reach out to them with the loving power of God, with the message of forgiveness and the hope of salvation.

We knew the desperation of failure, the disappointment of lost initiatives, the depression of rejection and insult. At last, we realised that we could do nothing on our own.

Then we found the joy of discovering that anything is possible when we fully depend on the Spirit, when we live in his presence and allow him to work through us.

Sometimes we have come across biblical truths which explained what we had already learnt in practice. At other times we went on our knees to God's word to find the solution to our weakness and sin.

I wrote this book because I was certain that the living God could use you to make a difference to some of the needy folk who live around you.

Most people I meet are desperate for a change, desperate for spiritual reality, desperate to make a difference. Now you know that the Spirit is always bringing decisive change so that believers can make a difference.

I have tried to introduce you to the mysterious person of the Holy Spirit. We have looked at him and his work throughout the Scriptures and have seen that he is God's power in action.

You have grasped that he brings power for proclamation, power for miracles and warfare, power for hope and perseverance, power for the church to witness.

Please don't forget that, in the Spirit, God's power is given so that you will be a powerful witness to the risen Lord Jesus. Every aspect of the power is given to enable you to know Jesus better and to help you reveal him more clearly to the needy world around you.

You should also have appreciated by now that the Holy Spirit is God's purity in person. Through the Spirit, God cleanses you from sin's pollution by helping you to resist temptation and do what is right.

The Spirit is God's agent of purity: through holy fire and water he is transforming you into the same image as Jesus. Why? So that the people around you can see the nature of Jesus and be drawn to him.

But the most wonderful truth you have found is that the Spirit brings the very presence of the Lord Jesus Christ to the church – to us, to me, to you.

It is the Spirit's most special work to make Jesus known, and he does this by making his home in human disciples, in you. Everything Jesus does is accomplished through the

Spirit. He speaks to you, he fellowships with you, he transforms you – by, through, in and with the Spirit.

Then Jesus calls you to reveal his presence, to speak his words, to do his deeds. All this is only possible because the Spirit is alongside you, is around you, is with you, is in you.

Since Pentecost, it has been the church's function to reveal God's great glory in and to the world. You and your local brothers and sisters have been chosen to show God's holy character to the people in your neighbourhood. Together, you are meant to be being seen as the place where God resides and you are supposed to be demonstrating God's regal authority and power.

You can only do it in the Spirit. You can only do it with the Spirit. But you can do it. You can make a difference.

Through the Spirit, Jesus is addressing and approaching you. He is urging you into powerful action – to deal with demons, to heal the broken-hearted, to feed the hungry, to go about doing just those one or two deeds he directs.

Through the Spirit, Jesus is drawing near to you. He is transforming you into a more pure way of living, shaping you into his own image.

And the Spirit is doing all this so that you can know Jesus better and make him better known.

Please don't resist the Spirit's holy work. Instead, as you close this book, please respond to him by actively submitting yourself to his will, by becoming his devoted partner – by starting to live always and only in his holy presence.